SECRETARY'S NEW GUIDE
TO DEALING WITH PEOPLE

SECRETARY'S NEW GUIDE TO DEALING WITH PEOPLE

Helen Norman Saputo
Nancy Gill Rutherford

Prentice Hall, Inc. Englewood Cliffs, New Jersey

Prentice-Hall International, Inc., *London*
Prentice-Hall of Australia, Pty. Ltd., *Sydney*
Prentice-Hall Canada, Inc., *Toronto*
Prentice-Hall of India Private Ltd., *New Delhi*
Prentice-Hall of Japan, Inc., *Tokyo*
Prentice-Hall of Southeast Asia Pte. Ltd., *Singapore*
Whitehall Books, Ltd., Wellington, *New Zealand*
Editora Prentice-Hall do Brasil Ltda., *Rio de Janeiro*
Prentice-Hall Hispanoamericana, S.A., *Mexico*

©1986 *by*

PRENTICE-HALL, INC.

Englewood Cliffs, N.J.

All rights reserved. No part of this
book may be reproduced in any form or
by any means, without permission in
writing from the publisher.

Library of Congress Cataloging-in-Publication Data

Saputo, Helen Norman
   Secretary's new guide to dealing with people.

   Includes index.
   1. Secretaries.   2. Office management.   3. Business
etiquette.   4. Interpersonal relations.   I. Rutherford,
Nancy Gill   II. Title.
HF5547.5.S27 1986   651.3′741   86-4888

ISBN 0-13-797382-9

Printed in the United States of America

Dedication

    This book is dedicated to our friend and artist, Betty Doyle Campbell, who contributed graphics to this book.

Acknowledgments

In order to be meaningful as a guide to the secretary in dealing with people, this book required the input of many people who are employed in the business setting.

We would particularly like to acknowledge the help of the following who read various portions of this manuscript:

Lawrence J. Finnegan, Acting Supreme Court Justice, Kings County, New York

Lila Friedman, Associate Professor, Business Department, Queensborough Community College, Bayside, New York

No book about secretaries would be complete without input from working secretaries.

So, our sincere thanks to:

Arlene Greenberg, Bayside, New York

Sharon Vaughn, Basking Ridge, New Jersey

The help of our friends at Classen Corporation, Stamford, Connecticut is very much appreciated:

René A. M. Classen, President

Charles Taibi, Vice President

Also, a special "thank you" to Clinton H. Rutherford, Ph.D., for his encouragement and support.

And lastly, to Vito Saputo, M.B.A., C.P.A., for his critical reading and re-reading of our manuscript and for his encouragement and advice and helpful suggestions, thank you.

Helen Norman Saputo
Nancy Gill Rutherford

Contents

A Preview of What This Book Will Do for You xi

First Impressions—Being an Image Maker * Identify the Problems * Action Steps You Can Take to Improve the Situation * Practicing Human Relations Is the Key * Identify the Problem * Points to Remember * Preventive Systems * Seeing that Things Get Done

1 Consider the Effect You Have on Others...................... 1

Assisting Yourself * Are You a Leader or a Follower? * Self-Motivating Factors—Achieving Success Through Goal Setting * Creating a New You * Your Copability Profile * Wrapping Up

2 Expanding Your Skills to Meet the Demands of the Changing Office 13

Manage More Effectively * Organization—Key to Getting the Job Done * Action Steps for Delegating * Supervising More Effectively * Managing Difficult Situations * Managing Situations and People * Be Innovative * Skillful Decision Making * Assert Yourself * Wrapping Up

3 Proven Techniques for Handling Callers 27

Setting the Tone * Hints for Creating a Receptive Atmosphere * Your Appearance Conveys the Image of the Firm * Good Planning Gets Things Done * First Impressions Count * Avoiding Conflicts * Handling Pressure * Patience Is Basic to Handling All Crisis Situations * Making Everyone Feel Special * Practical Tips for Screening Visitors * Common Sense Advice on Handling All Types of Visitors: Social, Business, the VIP, Salespeople * Often Overlooked Ways to Increase Your Effectiveness * Wrapping Up

4 Communicating Effectively on the Telephone.................. 50

Key Points * Practicing Good Human Relations on the Telephone Is Always Important * Screening Calls * Placing Calls * Tips on

Handling Telephone Calls: Improving Voice, Diction, and Manners * Key Points * Key Questions—How to Get the Caller to Talk * Hints to Improve Your Listening Skills * Remaining Calm Is a Key Element * Proper Handling of Telephone Messages * The Psychology Behind Name Recognition * Tips on Dealing with the Angry Caller * Take Control of the Situation * Don't Say Too Much * Who's Minding the Phone? * Get Help from the Experts * Set Up Procedures * Tips for Improving Your Effectiveness on the Telephone * Wrapping Up

5 Essentials for Improving Your Communications Skills 71

Your Letter Reflects Your Boss * Guidelines for Composing Letters * Be Positive in Your Approach * Improving Grammar Skills * Comma Usage * Spelling and Word Division * Clear Up the Confusion Over Quotation Marks * Model Letters * Proper Stationery Helps * Handling Mail * Improving Your Processing of Incoming Mail * Practical Tips on Handling the Mail * Hints on Handling the Contents * Personal Mail * Professional Mail * Bills and Statements * Advertisements and Circulars * Periodicals and Professional Publications * When the Boss is Away * Wrapping Up

6 Developing Skill in Oral Communication...................... 103

First Impressions Are Important * Key Factors for Effective Communication * Improve Your Human Relations Skills Through Oral Communication * How You Say It * Listening * Tips for Increasing Your Listening Skills * Body Language Communicates * Checklist to Improve Your Ability to Speak and Discuss * Key Points to Remember * Wrapping Up

7 Here's How to Get Along with Your Bosses..................... 112

Creating the Proper Atmosphere * Keys to Getting Along * Multiple Bosses * No Stereotypes Please * Teamwork Is Essential * Understanding the Woman Boss * Compromise Is Often Necessary * Understanding Is the Key to Getting Along * Coping with Difficult Situations * Being Assertive * Wrapping Up

8 Linking Your Employer to Others............................. 130

Smoothing the Way * Making Your Boss Look Good * Getting the Message Across * Developing a Positive Atmosphere * Showing Respect * Tips for Successful Liaison with Those You Supervise * Developing a Positive Atmosphere * Your Role as Liaison with Others * Wrapping Up

9 Increasing Your Effectiveness as a Supervisor 142

Motivating Your Staff * Job Descriptions Are Helpful * Lines of Authority * Theories of Management * Achieving Good Interpersonal Relationships with Your Assistants * Providing a Good Working Atmosphere * Time Management * Setting Priorities * Increase Your Efficiency with Checklists * Wrapping Up

CONTENTS

10 Focusing on the Public 157

Project an Attitude of Concerned Graciousness * Even-tempered Behavior Spreads Good Will * Tips on Greeting Visitors to Your Office * Tips on Dealing with the "Unexpected" * How to Avoid Unkept Appointments * Effective Screening of Telephone Calls Avoids Problems * Avoiding Conflicts * Wrapping Up

11 Better Management of Social Relationships 166

Balancing Work and Play * Social Relationships Are Essential * Socializing with the Boss * Socializing with Boss's Spouse * Socializing with Other Business Associates * Socializing with Friends * Socializing with Relatives * Choosing Friends * Choosing Social Activities * Managing Vacation Time * Traveling * Weekend, Holiday, and Evening Socializing * Married or Single * Key Factors in Planning Your Leisure Activities * Wrapping Up

12 Successful Participation in Office Social Life 178

Social Relationships with Customers and Clients * The Office Party * Participating in Group Activities...Company Clubs, Teams, Classes * Handling Collections for Gifts * Accepting Gifts—Do's and Don'ts * Wrapping Up

13 Strategies for Handling Tough Office Situations 188

Getting Along with Superiors * Cooperate with Co-workers * Be Courteous with Business Associates * Keeping Up to Date with Colleagues * Keep Your Relationships Businesslike * Dealing with Other Members of the Organization * Special Hints If Your Boss Is a Woman * Strategies for Dealing with Mature Workers * Dealing Effectively with Crises * Creating a Good Working Atmosphere * Checklist for Creating a Good Working Atmosphere * Asserting Yourself * Test Yourself—Can You Answer "Yes" to the Following Questions? * Dealing Effectively with Delicate Situations * How to Gain Acceptance Without Creating Resentment * Wrapping Up

14 Creating a More Attractive You 205

Being Charming * A Handshake Is Important * Improving Your Voice and Diction * Good Manners Are Basic to Your Success * Dressing for the Job * For Women, Makeup and Hairstyle Are Important * Eating the Right Foods * What About Fast Foods? * Exercise for Good Health * Getting Proper Rest * Setting Aside Time for Play * And Don't Forget... * Planning and Thinking Constructively * Wrapping Up

15 Achieving a Good Working Atmosphere 219

Providing a Cooperative Atmosphere * Maintaining an Attractive Office * Making the Reception Area "Receptive" * How to Have an Uncluttered Desk * Office Appearance Is Important * Practicing Good Human Relations * Dealing Effectively with Everyone * Handling Stressful Situations Competently * Helping to Avoid

Conflicts * Understanding the Scope of Responsibility * Exercising Discretion * Acting with Tact and Diplomacy * Handling Callers Properly * Communicating Effectively Both Orally and in Writing * Adding to Your Telephone Skills * Good Management of Office Social and Personal Relationships * But What About You? * Wrapping Up

Index **235**

A Preview of What This Book Will Do for You

The secretary holds a unique position and is a very special person. You may already know all the things that secretaries have always had to know—you must have top-notch skills, excellent knowledge of shorthand, typing, filing, and general clerical skills. You are a *super* receptionist and you have great telephone technique, but are you thoroughly prepared to meet the challenges of today's fast-paced office? Are you a specialist in interpersonal relationships? Can you deal with people effectively?

Decision-making and exercising initiative are integral parts of the necessary requirements for today's secretary/administrative assistant, but the value of these skills is diminished if you cannot get along with other people.

Advances in technology such as the introduction of word processing with its automated equipment are changing office structure and have expanded the role of the secretary. No longer does taking dictation and transcribing it consume a major portion of the secretary's day. Word processing equipment has left the secretary free to really become an assistant to the boss or to be the office manager; free to grow and exercise the supervisory and managerial skills so important in today's office.

Although automation has freed the secretary from much of the routine, repetitive work, the skill that automation cannot perform is the human relations skill—dealing with people.

Today, the business world is based more than ever on interaction among people. Changing technology has developed many new positions that in turn have led to many new combinations of interpersonal relationships.

The secretary who has developed skill in dealing with people will become a valuable asset to any firm and will find rewards in high salary and in personal satisfaction.

This book will help you meet this challenge. You will increase your ability to deal with people effectively. The practical ideas and suggestions presented will be immediately useful in your everyday office situation. You will recognize many problem situations that you have encountered in your office and you will benefit from the solutions presented.

Anticipating and knowing how to cope with the many situations that can develop in the office environment will help you enormously in your job.

This easy-to-read, handy guide to dealing with people will provide you with hundreds of practical tips. You will feel that you are identifying with others while discovering new ways to expand your skills. Here are 20 ways this book will help. You will find out how to:

1. convey the image of your firm
2. keep clients happy on the telephone
3. improve your decision-making skills
4. be an effective supervisor
5. get along with a high-pressure executive
6. cope with problems created by the new technology
7. delegate tasks effectively
8. be the office diplomat
9. find new ways to organize effectively
10. communicate successfully with co-workers
11. solve tough office situations
12. manage more than one boss at a time

13. balance social and office life
14. avoid the "fast food" syndrome
15. write better letters
16. cope with stress
17. use body language to improve communication
18. communicate through listening
19. express yourself more effectively
20. use checklists to increase your efficiency

You have an extremely important job—you represent your company and your boss. The way that you present yourself will often have a significant effect on the way that the people with whom you deal see your company and your boss.

FIRST IMPRESSIONS—BEING AN IMAGE MAKER

The secretary reflects the image of the company. A gracious, caring, but businesslike secretary conveys the message that the company is concerned about the interests of its customers or clients and will treat them in a fair, honest and knowledgeable way. Often you are the first person a client or customer sees and if the image you portray is not a good one, your company will probably lose business. You may be a very competent secretary, but if the image you portray is one of a harried, confused, disorganized person, the customer may see the entire business as disorganized and not one that is interested in serving his/her welfare. If, however, the customer's first impression of you is a good one, then the business will also look good. The client or customer needs to feel he is the most important person at that particular time.

For example:

> You are secretary to the president of a word processing consulting firm. The office is extremely busy. Work is constantly being delivered to your desk from the Word Processing Center and the Reprographics Department. The office staff is continually coming to you to report or to receive new assignments. At times the situation becomes very hectic. Your company is a consulting firm. The clients

who come in are interested in improving their own offices so it is extremely important that you appear calm and efficient.

IDENTIFY THE PROBLEMS

You need to analyze the situation and clearly identify the problem areas so that you can take action.

1. Having a lot of work delivered to your desk can look very confusing to a visitor even though you are well able to handle it.
2. If the office staff is continually coming to your desk a caller will feel that your attention is divided between what he (the caller) is saying to you and what you must do in order to deal with your assistants.

Point to Remember: The caller in this situation wants your undivided attention and also wants to feel that the work of the office is getting accomplished.

ACTION STEPS YOU CAN TAKE TO IMPROVE THE SITUATION

1. If it is imperative that work be delivered to you and not to another area of the office:
   a. reorganize the physical set-up around your section of the office.
   b. set up an area behind a divider or a screen where work can be delivered.
2. If the office staff must receive their assignments from you:
   a. set up a system of trays or folders or mailboxes behind this screened area for each of these people so that they can easily drop off reports, leave memos with questions, and pick up instructions.
   b. select a convenient time slot for picking up most assignments or delivering reports if necessary. Of course,

anything of an emergency nature could be handled at any time but this would cut down on the constant coming and going and limit most of it to specific times.

Of course all situations are different and you can make adjustments according to your own particular needs, but the following *action steps* will help in any situation.

1. Analyze the situation.
2. Identify the problem(s). There may be more than one problem when at first you thought there was only one.
3. Outline suggested solutions.
4. Seek the cooperation of others. When the solutions affect your employer and/or other members of the staff, present the problem and the solution to your employer for approval and discuss it with the members of the staff involved. Give the reasons for whatever changes are being made. They will then be willing to cooperate. *Remember,* without cooperation, the best of plans can fail.
5. Be flexible. Try the solution. If it does not work out, be willing to make adjustments.

Checklists containing hints, tips, actions steps, and so forth are provided throughout as an aid to help you improve your ability to organize your time and tasks more efficiently. For example, a checklist for solving problems appears below.

PRACTICING HUMAN RELATIONS IS THE KEY

In order to provide the proper image of your company and your boss, you need to be very effective in your dealings with people. The human relations side of your job is very important and being constantly aware of and sensitive to the needs and reactions of those with whom you are dealing is the key to being effective.

> For example: you have just arrived at your desk. You are a little late because there was an enormous traffic jam on the highway, your car overheated, and you had to pull over to

DATE 7/2

CHECKLIST FOR _Solving Problems_

NOTES & COMMENTS _Too much activity around desk — work delivered, people coming etc._

- [x] 1. Analyze the Situation
- [x] 2. Identify the Problem(s)
- [ ] 3. Outline Solution
- [ ] 4. Seek Cooperation < bass / others
- [ ] 5. Try Solution
- [ ] 6. Make Adjustments
- [ ] 7.
- [ ] 8.
- [ ] 9.
- [ ] 10.

A PREVIEW OF WHAT THIS BOOK WILL DO FOR YOU xvii

the side of the road and wait until it cooled down and the traffic let up. There is a customer waiting who immediately starts to reprimand you because he has been waiting to see your boss for 15 minutes. He is a very busy person and does not see that there is any excuse for his having to wait.

IDENTIFY THE PROBLEM

The customer is really being irrational and unfair in his statements, and has not even let you catch your breath as you arrive at your desk. He is wrong to attack you verbally in this manner, and you feel like answering him the same way. But, should you? Will it help you? Will it make you feel better? But, more important, will it keep this customer or will it drive his business away and perhaps cause him to mention the matter to other prospective customers? He must be calmed down diplomatically, so that he forgets that he had to wait.

POINTS TO REMEMBER

The important thing to remember is that you cannot worry too much about your own feelings—whether the person is right or wrong—but, rather, how you are going to deal with the situation, and keep the disgruntled callers as customers of your business. This requires that you exercise tact and diplomacy in many instances and, in the long run, will pay big dividends in creating a better atmosphere of cooperation between you and your client.

The *problem* in this case is how to calm down this customer and keep his business. He really does not want to hear a lot of excuses. So the solution is probably simply to say: "I am very sorry, please let me help you now."

PREVENTIVE SYSTEMS

Another thought may be to set up a preventive system in your office to take care of situations such as this, because emergencies do happen. One idea might be to work out a "buddy-system" with another secretary so that if either one of you is not in on time, the other will check to see if a client is waiting and apologize, saying something like:

> Ms. James is not in yet; she must have been unavoidably delayed and not been able to call in. May I help you?

Most people will be reasonable in a case like this. What annoys most of us is being ignored. Everyone knows that emergencies do occur. This way, with a "preventive problem solver" you diffuse a situation before it becomes a problem.

SEEING THAT THINGS GET DONE

As a secretary you have the unique role of being a prime mover in your business. You are responsible for seeing that things get done. Your boss gives you instructions that more often than not require you to deal with others both in written and oral communication. You may have to write letters or telephone people or speak to them in person. Often the matters with which you are entrusted are of a delicate nature and your employer wants results.

> Your employer may ask you to straighten out a situation that is developing among a group of clerical workers. They are mostly students who work on a part-time basis and come to work directly from school wearing the clothing they wear in school, which is inappropriate for your office. Your boss is not particularly interested in how easy or difficult the task assigned you is, only in the results. Some of these people are not interested in doing what you want them to, or feel that it is an imposition to require them to dress as others in the office do. They cannot wear their good clothing to school, and they do not have time to change before coming to work. They are very annoyed that the matter was even brought up. No one mentioned it when they were hired. In fact, they may even quit if they have to dress differently. The workers in question are quite efficient and you need them, so you must solve this

problem. Your boss will not like it if they leave, but your boss will not like it if they continue to dress the way they do. How would you handle this problem?

In Chapter 2, we will discuss some suggested solutions, but right now think about what you would do about this and other problems, such as the following:

> An older worker, who has been with the company for many years, works with a group of younger women and feels that because of the age differential and her seniority that she can "boss" them around. They resent it. She is a valued employee but she is causing problems with the younger workers. Your office cannot run efficiently with such situations. You must deal with them. You cannot go running to your boss and ask for help. It is now your problem. How will you handle it?

Another problem that is common in an office has to do with division of responsibility.

> Certain reports are due at particular times. Your boss has asked you to see that they are submitted on time. You go to the people responsible and find that "the buck gets passed." One person cannot do his job until someone else does his and so forth. Again, you have the responsibility of "seeing that things get done." What do you do? (Look for the solution in Chapter 2.)

These are just a few examples of common problems that we all encounter as secretaries. There are many solutions, but one thing is sure, the problems must be solved and in order to do so you need to be skilled in the practice of good human relations and know how to deal with people effectively. It is your responsibility to see that the good of your company comes before your personal needs or desires. Once the problems are *identified* and you are aware of where the *focus* for the *solution* lies, you are on the road to *resolving* the situation.

In the fifteen chapters that follow, we have endeavored to provide a blueprint for today's secretary/assistant, based on principles that have worked in the classroom and have been tested and proven effective in the work world. Whatever the business or professional setting in which you are employed, whatever the education and special skills required, the foundation of your achievement rests on your ability to deal successfully with other people. Let these principles and methods work for you and you will reach your goals and objectives, with and through others.

Helen Norman Saputo
Nancy Gill Rutherford

1

Consider the Effect You Have on Others

Being aware of everything that is going on around you, being sensitive to another person's feelings, understanding people and knowing why they feel certain ways or do certain things is of extreme importance in dealing with people. But, do not forget yourself. Ask yourself these questions.

Who are you?

What are you like?

What are your weaknesses and strengths?

Are you nervous? Calm? High-strung? Low-keyed?

Do you like to work under pressure or are you happier when working at a slower pace?

In other words, knowing yourself involves being able to understand other people so that you can deal with them effectively. This all hinges on what kind of person *you* are.

For example:

> Janet is a very vivacious, high-powered type of person—she works well under pressure and performs her best when she has a deadline to meet. She very rarely starts a job early even though she knows that it is coming up.
>
> Janet has responsibility for getting out the office newsletter every month. She sets aside the last week of the month

to do this and runs around gathering information from people and getting them to re-do news items they have submitted. Janet is exhilarated. She loves this and this would be fine except that many other people are involved and tempers often become short because the others see no reason to be pressured this way. They are willing to help out in a emergency but do not see this "monthly emergency" as necessary. The work could be spaced out during the month. Consequently, Janet is getting fewer and fewer contributions to the newsletter.

She feels that it is because the other people are not willing to cooperate even though she has explained the situation to them and asked for their cooperation. She feels that she does all the right things in dealing with people—she does not show anger or reprimand anyone but explains everything.

What she does not realize is that she is causing trouble by not being aware of traits in her that irritate others. This is an "emergency" that Janet has created because she prefers to work this way, but it is not a *real* emergency. The work could be spread over the month and not crammed into the last week. A "deadline" does not *have* to mean pressure.

So you must learn about yourself and develop your personality. The first step would be to identify your own personality traits or type. Are you like any of these secretaries? Do you see yourself in any of the following situations?

Margaret is a "morning" person. She arrives at the office 45 minutes early every morning after having had a good breakfast and accomplishing chores at home. She is "raring to go." All her tasks are lined up and she sets right to work. Whatever work she must delegate is ready to be handed over with full instructions as soon as the people arrive. Margaret has everything planned perfectly and her only holdup at times is the fact that the people with whom she works are not always as ready and able to accomplish as quickly as she can in the morning.

Linda is a "late-starter." She arrives at her desk on time but anyone who knows her realizes that she needs her second cup of coffee (which she brings in with her) before she can really get started on the day's work. This can be very irritating to Margaret who needs some cooperation from her and finds she has to wait for it until after the coffee is finished. Margaret has been at her desk early and so the wait appears longer than it actually is. Linda does not see why she has to be "jumped on" the minute she walks in—so the two women sometimes start the day off wrong.

Anna is very ambitious. She is an excellent secretary. She majored in secretarial studies at the local junior college and is now taking management courses in the evening. She is anxious to be promoted to a supervisory position as soon as one opens up. Anna loves her work and wants to do a good job. Over lunch she always talks to the other secretaries about how much she would like to be promoted to the secretarial supervisor's position when it opens up and about how well qualified she is becoming with all the courses she is taking. Anna often skips her coffee break because she wants to get her work done as quickly and well as possible so that she will be noticed for the opening when it occurs.

However, Anna does not realize that she is becoming less and less liked by the other secretaries. After all, some of them are interested in promotions also. They dislike her skipping her coffee breaks because they think it "shows them up." They are no longer as anxious to cooperate with her on any joint efforts as they were. Anna is so ambitious for herself that she does not realize that she is hurting the feelings of the other secretaries.

This certainly is not helping her to be considered for promotion to a supervisory position if she is not able to deal with the people with whom she works.

Patricia is a perfectionist—everything she does is done beautifully. She plans each task and performs it perfectly. She is conscientious about everything she does. She approaches everything in a systematic and thorough manner. In order to have everything meet her standards of perfection, she must control the situation. Naturally, as a top-level secretary, she cannot do every job herself. A big portion of her job is to supervise others and delegate work.

Unfortunately (or perhaps fortunately), not everyone is the perfectionist she is. She often becomes irritated with her co-workers because they do not work up to her standards.

Her co-workers become irritated with her because they are not perfectionists and consider her standards unrealistic and often wasteful of time.

Are you anything like "Margaret, the morning person," "Linda, the late starter," "Ambitious Anna," or "Patricia, the perfectionist." Maybe you are not exactly like any of these people, but perhaps you recognize some of these same traits in yourself and others.

It is important to realize that even good traits can be irritating to others and we must learn to recognize not only what we are like but how we affect those around us.

Make a "Rate Yourself Chart" (see figure 1-1) to develop your own "personal" personality profile. The following list of traits will be helpful to you in developing your "Personality Profile." Perhaps you can think of others that you may want to use.

PERSONALITY TRAITS

involved	interested	dedicated
sensitive	aware	attentive
respectful	motivated	self-starter
responsible	thorough	cooperative
sympathetic	considerate	calm
cheerful	neat	attractive
pleasant	friendly	warm
courteous	conscientious	patient
outgoing	orderly	organized
dependable	honest	ethical
punctual	loyal	mannerly
efficient	poised	tactful
mature	flexible	determined
idealistic	perceptive	influencing
adaptable	persistent	ambitious
farseeing	anticipating	caring

CONSIDER THE EFFECT YOU HAVE ON OTHERS

Now try again. How do these traits affect other people? Make believe that you are one of your co-workers, who is rating you. Well, fun or not, it forces you to do something that is extremely important in learning about yourself—you actually start to think about how others see you.

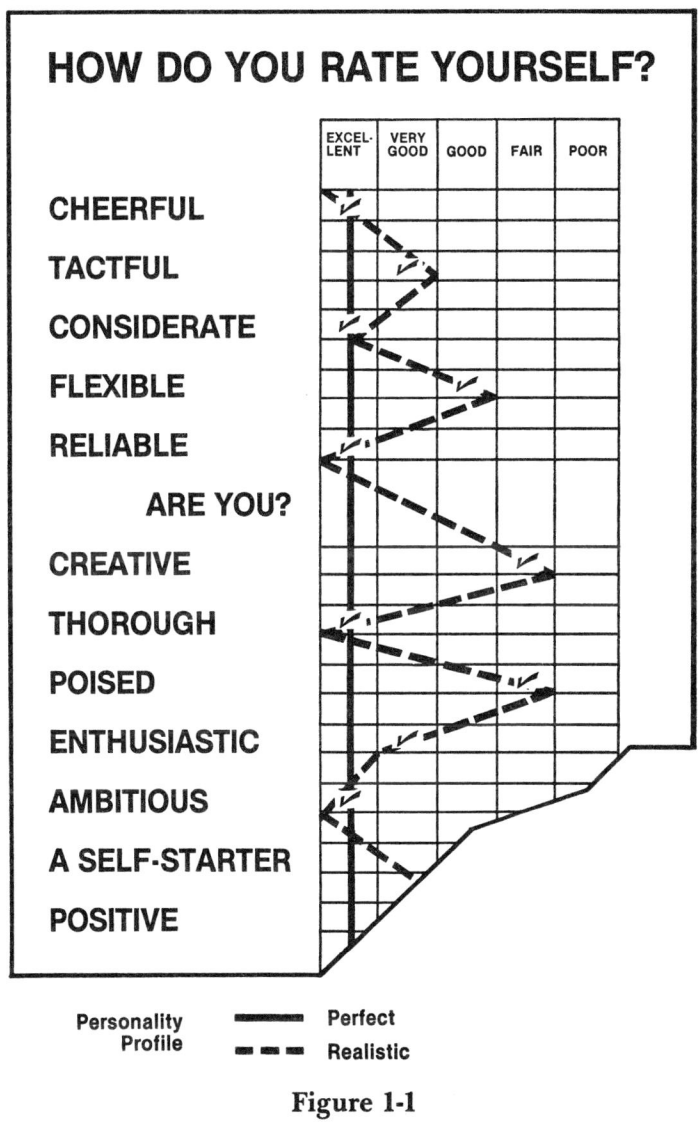

Figure 1-1

Be careful—try to be honest in your approach. You may not look at things honestly and feel that people see you exactly as wonderful as you think you are, or even more of a danger, you may be so sensitive that you start thinking that no one is happy with your personality.

The main thing to be aware of is that when two personalities are involved, even if both are good, they may adversely affect each other. You cannot control the other person, but if you can recognize the problem, you may be able to adjust *your* behavior.

For example, *Margaret,* "the morning person," should be aware that all of the people with whom she works are not as chipper in the morning as she is, so she should direct her energies on things she can control, not on what others must do for her. For *Margaret's* work to hinge on something *Linda,* "the late starter," has to do immediately is not productive. Know your people and arrange the work you need to do with them for times that will be productive for both of you. Have another job you can work on while you wait for *Linda* to have her coffee. Perhaps *Margaret* could say something like "Good morning *Linda,* I have to run down to the mail room. When I get back after you have had your coffee, could we work on this project. I have everything written out and I'll leave it with you now and go over it with you before you start. Thanks."

This way *Linda* has been alerted that there is something that must be done right away, but knows *Margaret* is not standing over her shoulder waiting. *Linda* is a good worker and the job will get done on time, and she will still have her coffee. *Margaret* is taking care of another project so that she will not feel the time is wasted.

In the above problem, *Margaret* has de-emphasized the negative effect her positive trait of starting early has on a late starter by utilizing her time effectively during her wait to work with *Linda.*

ASSISTING YOURSELF

Think about your own personality and how you can make it work to accomplish the best for you.

What are your positive traits?

What are your negative traits?
How do these traits affect others?
How can you de-emphasize the negative traits?
How can you accentuate your positive traits?
Can you accept your own personality traits?

ARE YOU A LEADER OR A FOLLOWER?

We must take this into account when we "learn about ourselves." It takes both leaders and followers to accomplish the tasks at hand. A leader is one who can influence others to work toward attaining set goals. There are three factors that bear on one's ability to exercise leadership:

1. *Personality*—how we relate to others
2. *Ability*—some are just "born" leaders
3. *Authority*—may be bestowed by one's title or by one's position

As people's personalities differ, so do styles of leadership. Likewise companies have different philosophies of how things should be run. The three most common leadership styles[1] are:

1. *Authoritarian*—The leader makes all decisions, orders, and expects them to be carried out.
2. *Democratic*—The leader invites participation from the group. Decisions usually made after consultation with the members of the group.
3. *Laissez-faire (subordinate-centered)*—The leader gives general objectives and guidelines for subordinates to follow, but is not directly involved with the group unless requested. This type of leadership is often found to be frustrating and the group sometimes feels there is no leadership at all.

FACTORS THAT INFLUENCE LEADERSHIP

1. Title or position
2. Appearance

---

[1]Howell, William C. and Dipboye, Robert L., *Essentials of Industrial and Organizational Psychology*, The Dorsey Press, 1982, pp. 136-140.

3. Type of business
4. Willingness of group to be led
5. Knowledge and natural ability

CHECKLIST OF HINTS ON HOW TO IMPROVE YOUR OWN LEADERSHIP SKILLS

1. Experience—Past experiences will enhance your effectiveness.

2. Education—Courses in human relations, management, psychology, speech, and communications (written and oral) are helpful.

3. Seminars and workshops—The time span is usually brief (a day or two) and the focus is on one subject so that there is a high degree of concentration.

4. Leadership development programs—These can be workshop or seminar format, or college courses.

5. Personal Development—Read as widely as possible from books and current periodicals on the subject.

6. Membership in professional organizations—You will meet others of like interests and ambition and you will form friendships that can eventually lead to a network of people who share their problems as well as help each other out when a need arises.

ESSENTIALS OF EFFECTIVE LEADERSHIP

1. Good human relations skills
2. Ability to organize
3. Ability to get cooperation from others
4. Hard work
5. Sensitivity

SELF-MOTIVATING FACTORS—ACHIEVING SUCCESS THROUGH GOAL SETTING

Goal setting is an important motivational factor in achieving what you want. It gives direction to your life, stimulates you

DATE 6/6

CHECKLIST FOR Improving Leadership Skills

NOTES & COMMENTS Things I need or have

- ☑ 1. Experience – Faculty Workshop last year
- ☑ 2. Education – Management Course
- ☑ 3. Seminar – (ABC - Corp)
- ☑ 4. LDP – Look for one
- ☑ 5. Subscription to Management Mag.
- ☑ 6. Join an Organization
- ☐ 7.
- ☐ 8.
- ☐ 9.
- ☐ 10.

Figure 1-2

to work toward the achievement of something, and increases your chances for success and personal satisfaction.

> Barbara has been working as a secretary to three lawyers for two years. They like her and she likes the job, and now that she "knows the ropes" so to speak, the job has become somewhat routine and boring because Barbara is very efficient, a good manager, and would like something more challenging.
>
> The firm is expanding its word processing department and there will be openings for assistant supervisors and supervisor/managers. Barbara's goal might be to become an assistant supervisor and then move up to supervisor, and on to manager.

Most of us are familiar with setting short-term goals like listing things you want to "Do Today," and as Alan Lakin, author and expert on time management, stresses, put your goals in order of priority and stick to your list. Start with the most important items first and end with those things that can be postponed until later. As you accomplish each task and check it off, your sense of self-satisfaction will be greatly increased. It is almost like giving yourself a pat on the back.

Begin with daily work goals. Set up a list of duties to be accomplished each day. Then aim for longer-term goals. Barbara's long-term goals are career goals. She is planning where she wants to be five to ten years down the road. By actually writing down a list of career objectives, she will focus her attention on the direction in which she wants her job to lead and can direct all her energy to that end.

Sometimes personal goals influence one's career goals. For instance, suppose you prefer to work near your home in order to save commuting time and expense. This will naturally affect your career goals.

The following list of Barbara's career goals[2] may give you some insight into how to go about defining your own career objectives.

---

[2]These goals could include a time element with each one. However, that would be subject to many factors. Barbara might even include in her goals the possibility of moving to another firm in order to advance.

CONSIDER THE EFFECT YOU HAVE ON OTHERS

1. Secretary to attorneys
2. Secretary to one of the partners in the firm
3. Coordinator of document production/word processing
4. Supervisor of Word Processing Department
5. Manager of Office Services

CREATING A NEW YOU

By learning about yourself and dealing with some of the positives and negatives of your personality, you are on the road to creating a new you and developing your full potential. A large part of this is your ability to cope with all kinds of situations, which in your every day dealings with people, becomes a never ending part of your job.

YOUR COPABILITY PROFILE

Think of the things with which you have to cope day in and day out. Make a list similar to the illustration in figure 1-3 and rate yourself. What is *your* Copability Index?

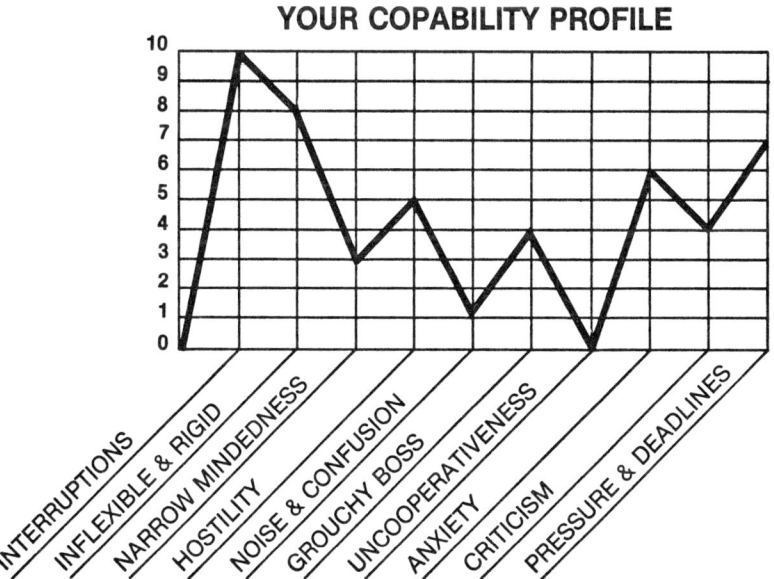

Figure 1-3

Where do you fit in? Are you a "5" or do you hit highs on certain items, say, "inflexible" you are an "8", but on interruptions you shoot up to "10." Wouldn't it be better if you could learn to deal with the everyday stresses and maintain a low profile in the range of "2 to 5" with an occasional lapse? Take a look at your own copability profile to see how you stack up.

WRAPPING UP

Learning about yourself is not an easy task, nor is it one that you can do once and then say it is done. It is an on-going process. We change daily as we grow and mature in our personal relationships. It is never easy, nor is it pleasant, to recognize our negative traits, but we can. We must also realize that our positive traits can have a negative effect on others. Growth is a gradual process of change that occurs as you continue to learn about yourself.

2

Expanding Your Skills to Meet the Demands of the Changing Office

The duties of the secretary are many and varied. Of course, you have all the technical skills necessary for the job—stenography, typing, filing, spelling, grammar, and punctuation, and, today, in many instances, knowledge of computers, data processing, and word processing. In addition to being the efficient, competent professional secretary demanded by today's business, you must have even more than that. You must also see that things get done; become a better manager; organize the tasks for which you are responsible in order to make the most of the time available and do the most effective job; delegate tasks to others; supervise those to whom you delegate jobs; be innovative in your approach to both your job and the people with whom you deal; be as much of a diplomat in your office contacts as if you were employed in government diplomatic service; develop your decision-making skills; and know how to apply decision-making models to achieve logical thinking. You must always keep an open mind and be continually ready to learn new things. You provide the picture of the organization for which you work; people see you as a reflection of your boss and the organization. Make sure the picture they see is a good one and a true reflection.

MANAGE MORE EFFECTIVELY

In order to effectively manage your many and varied responsibilities, know exactly what they are. A good tip is to periodically review and update the tasks under your management by preparing job descriptions of both your own job and the jobs of others that do work for you. Your company personnel office may have these job descriptions on each employee—obtain copies and review and update them. The personnel department, in this case, will probably be able to supply you with blank forms, also. If these forms are not available and your office does not have job descriptions already prepared, then you may have to start the process. (See figure 2-1 Sample General Job Description for An Administrative Assistant and figure 2-2 Job Description prepared by you, as secretary, for a junior secretary under your supervision.)

ORGANIZATION—THE KEY TO GETTING THE JOB DONE

Being a good organizer is a very important key to success in any of life's endeavors and, of course, it is of prime importance to the secretary. If you cannot organize your time and your tasks effectively, you will be confused and will not be able to think and act effectively. There are many facets to your day and you must be able to move quickly from one thing to another. If you are disorganized, it will be immediately noticeable to those with whom you deal and even though you may know how to practice good human relations, the atmosphere you have created around you will negate your good intentions. For example:

> You have a hundred and one things to do today; there is a group of salesmen from all over the state coming in for a

EXPANDING YOUR SKILLS 15

JOB DESCRIPTION

TITLE OF JOB Administrative Assistant

JOB REQUIREMENTS (training, skills, and/or experience)

Organizational ability, smooth handling of many and varied details, and a self starter.

3–5 years of experience, preferably in an administrative area

Excellent skills—typing—60 wpm. and steno required.

TASKS PERFORMED
1. Handles telephones
2. Handle mail—sorting, annotating, routing
3. Greet and screen visitors
4. Schedules appointments and remind executive of appointments
5. Take dictation
6. Compose routine correspondence
7. Proofread and edit copy
8. Delegate tasks
9. Maintain and organize records for quick access
10. Schedule and arrange for conferences and meetings
11. Research and gather information for articles, speeches, etc.
12. Systematize office work flow
13. Supervise secretarial assistant

Figure 2-1

seminar. You have to arrange to greet them, introduce them, and get the mechanics of the seminar running smoothly. But you also have your everyday responsibilities to take care of. In the pressure of things you become confused and overlook some important duties such as submitting the attendance report to personnel. Personnel calls you at the seminar asking what happened to the report and would you submit it right away. This adds to your pressure and you get more confused, thus setting the scene for more overlooked duties.

You should keep a check list of things to do every day and not rely on memory. Write it down and check it off (see figure 2-3). This leaves your mind free and uncluttered, thus creating an atmosphere conducive to the practice of good human relations.

JOB DESCRIPTION

Name *Doris Young*
Job Title *Jr. Secretary*
Training *High School*
Duties *Telephone*
Receptionist
Schedule Appts.
Mail
File Stens
Typing 45-50 wpm.

Date *6/7* Signature *Uno*

Figure 2-2

EXPANDING YOUR SKILLS 17

DATE _5/9_

CHECKLIST FOR _Housekeeping_

NOTES & COMMENTS _Daily   D ✓_
Weekly   W
Monthly M

- ☑ 1. _Air office_
- ☑ 2. _Check Reception Area_
- ☑ 3. _Check Answering Service_
- ☐ 4. _Follow-up file_
- ☐ 5. _In-basket_
- ☐ 6.
- ☐ 7.
- ☐ 8.
- ☐ 9.
- ☐ 10.

Figure 2-3

A sample checklist of duties may include the following:

CHECKLIST OF DUTIES

Air Office
    Check air temperature and adjust

Check reception area for neatness
    See that all magazines are current
    See that all ashtrays are emptied and clean
    Turn calendars to current date
    Water plants and dust

Check employer's office

Sharpen pencils and see that pens are available

Check to see that maintenance staff has performed all housekeeping duties required

Check answering service

Check in-basket and organize

Check follow-up file for today's jobs and follow through

Prepare necessary reports

ACTION STEPS FOR DELEGATING

Delegating tasks is very important. You cannot feel that the only job well done is the job you do yourself. You must be able to release certain tasks to others. Remember, though, that releasing jobs to others only releases the work, not the responsibility. That stays with you. Be very careful to develop the skills necessary to help you in choosing the right people to do the jobs. Then, once a job is delegated, just see that it is done accurately and promptly. Do not hover over the person or nag. For example:

> Your boss is away from the office and has left the following instructions for you on a cassette:
>
> > 1. You are to contact the president of the company and inform him that your boss has been called away on a

personal emergency and will not be able to attend the staff meeting at 11 o'clock, but will send the requested report.

2. You are to contact the accounting department and get some new figures to be included in the report needed for the meeting.

3. You are to edit the report and type it for the meeting and prepare 20 copies in folders labeled with the name of each meeting participant.

4. You are to retype and include with the report three letters that your boss has corrected.

You have only an hour and a half to do this. Some work must be delegated, but which?

Call the president yourself and explain your bosses' absence. This is not a delegated task. The president will not think well of the absence if it is explained by anyone other than the confidential assistant, you.

Contact the accounting department and request the figures—for the same reason—you are passing on your bosses' request. You have the authority to do this.

Edit the report and perhaps retype it with the new figures from the accounting department—but your assistant can be retyping the three corrected letters and preparing the folders and labels. She will also make the 20 copies of the report and include them with the three retyped letters in the folders.

Check everything and be responsible for the total package. See that it gets to the meeting on time.

Your boss has delegated you to take care of this. You have delegated some portions to your assistant. *Remember,* you can only delegate work, not responsibility, so you must be very careful what and to whom you delegate—but you must always think in terms of delegating. In the above example, had you not delegated, you would not have been able to get the job done on time.

SUPERVISING MORE EFFECTIVELY

Along with delegating jobs to others comes the need to supervise. Which brings you back to "square one." In order to be an effective supervisor you must get along well with the people you supervise. They do not have to love you as a friend, but they have to have the respect for you and your abilities that will make them want to do the job for you. They have to feel that the job they are doing is important and that you have confidence in their ability to get the job done; that they can call on you for help, and that you understand the work and are fair in your assignments.

MANAGING DIFFICULT SITUATIONS

All of your duties as a secretary require managerial skills. You must be a good manager—of time, of tasks, of people, and of your emotions. In dealing with people in all kinds of situations, you are called on to be in complete control of your emotions at all times. You may be very worried about a personal problem you have, but you cannot allow that to affect the way you treat the people with whom you deal in your business situation. Too many people carry personal problems to work. On the other hand your employer may come to work unusually grumpy and unfairly reprimand you for something. You know that this is wrong, but it would be unwise to answer back in kind. Nothing will be accomplished and your employer will only become further annoyed with you. If you find a tactful way to handle the situation, your boss will realize that you are right even though he/she may not say so in words. Remember, often people act unfairly and irrationally under stress and emotion, and if you exert a calming influence they will become aware that they are being unfair in their reactions. But, if you in turn react harshly, more antagonism will develop. Being able to be the diplomat in all situations is an invaluable asset for any secretary.

MANAGING SITUATIONS AND PEOPLE

You, in your position as secretary, should always be aware of better, more interesting, more effective, and more efficient ways to approach the various jobs in your office. Do not be

EXPANDING YOUR SKILLS 21

afraid of change. We often do things the same way over and over again, approaching all situations the same way without recognizing that times and perspectives change, and we should be looking into more innovative ways to accomplish our various duties.

Perhaps a solution to the earlier problem of the clerical workers coming to work in casual school attire (see Introduction p. xviii) would be to suggest that the company provide colorful, attractive smocks to wear over their clothes. *Remember,* when calling the problem to the attention of the clerical workers, be very careful not to offend them. Another solution might be to provide a locker room or lounge area where the workers can change their clothing or perhaps leave an appropriate outfit at the office.

Maybe, in the case of the older worker who is causing trouble with the younger workers (see Introduction p. xix), a solution could be arrived at if the younger people were given the opportunity to discuss their resentment freely with you and you were able to tell them a little of the situation with the older worker. Perhaps a luncheon or coffee meeting with all of you would help. This is a situation where diplomacy and tact are so very important.

BE INNOVATIVE

An innovative approach to the division of responsibility or "buck-passing" situation (see Introduction p. xix) may be to work with the people involved, telling them that it is your responsibility to get this work done for your employer and you just can't do it without their help, so maybe you could all work together setting up a checklist or timetable of tasks. Have each person briefly describe the tasks they do and the date of expected completion of these tasks (see figure 2-4 Timetable of Tasks). After receiving the timetable from each employee, set up a worksheet for combining tasks (see figure 2-5). When the final checklist is set up, distribute copies to everyone involved including your employer (see figure 2-6 Master List of Tasks Performed). In this manner, each will know his responsibility

TIME TABLE OF TASKS

Name: Teresa Saputo Dept: Personnel Supervisor: John Clinton

Job Title: Personnel Assistant

Tasks Performed	Special Conditions of Performance	DAILY	WEEKLY	MONTHLY	SEMIANNUALLY	YEARLY
1. Xeroxing						
2. Telephone						
3. File						
4. Recruitment						
5. Mailing lists						
6.						
7.						
8.						
9.						
10.						
11.						
12.						

Figure 2-4

EXPANDING YOUR SKILLS 23

WORK SHEET FOR COMBINING TASKS

Employee _David Reade_
Dept. _Personnel_
Supervisor _John Clinton_

TASKS

1. Sets up appmts. with new applicants
2. Telephones prospective employers ✓
3. Arranges evaluation confs. with employees
4. Schedules orientations for supervisors ✓
5. Reviews applications
6. Maintains mailing list ✓

Employee _Teresa Saputo_
Dept. _Personnel_
Supervisor _John Clinton_

TASKS

1. Xeroxing
2. Telephones prospective employers ✓
3. Maintains files ✓
4. Recruitment of new employees ✓
5. Telephoning supervisors
6. Updates mailing list ✓

Employee _Susan Murphy_
Dept. _Personnel_
Supervisor _John Clinton_

TASKS

1. Recruiting new employees ✓
2. Reviewing applications ✓
3. Telephones supervisors ✓
4. Schedules orientations for Supervisors ✓
5. Arranges for meetings & conferences
6. Maintains files

Figure 2-5

MASTER LIST OF TASKS PERFORMED

Department Personnel

Employee David Reade

TASKS

Sets up appmts. with new applicants
Reviews applications
Telephones prospective employees
Maintains and updates mailing list

Employee Teresa Saputo

TASKS

Xeroxing
Maintains files
Recruitment of new employees
Telephone supervisors
Follow-up evaluation of new employees

Supervisor John Clinton

Employee Susan Murphy

TASKS

Schedules orientations for Supervisors
Responsible for all meetings and conferences (reserving rooms, setting up, speakers)
Typing agendas, programs,
Liaison with advertising agency

Figure 2-6

EXPANDING YOUR SKILLS

and each will know that the boss is also aware of this and will recognize each employee's work. If you have the availability of a computer you might want to adapt this project.

SKILLFUL DECISION MAKING

All of the above problems and their solutions, as well as the many other problems you encounter in your day-to-day business life, require decisions. Skill in decision-making is very important to the successful secretary. You must analyze each problem quickly and thoroughly, decide on what decisions to make, choose one based on good thinking, and be willing to stand by your decision. However, *keep an open mind,* because a decision can be changed or modified if the situation changes.

KEY QUESTIONS TO GUIDE YOU IN MAKING YOUR DECISION

1. What *decision* do I have to make?
2. What *choices* do I have?
3. What are my *strengths? Weaknesses?*
4. What is *most important* to get the job done? or What are my *priorities?*
5. Do I have all the *necessary information* I need to make a decision?
6. Do I need *more information?*
7. In choosing a solution, have I *considered the risks involved?*
   a. What are the *possible negative results?*
   b. What are the *possible positive results?*
8. *Based on what I know now, what is the best solution?*

ASSERT YOUSELF

In order to get along with people, you do not have to subordinate yourself to them, but you must be careful not to be overly aggressive or "pushy." You must assert yourself in a positive but pleasant way. See what the problem is and decide how to solve it. For example:

> Your boss constantly calls you in for dictation late in the afternoon, even though both of you have free time in the morning. This habit creates a rush situation every afternoon and a backlog of work held over for the next morning.
>
> The problem could be avoided if the dictation time were moved earlier in the day. You can say nothing about this situation and suffer, you can complain to your boss, or you can present an alternate plan to your boss explaining how much more efficient it would be to set aside an earlier hour for dictation. All the work would get out that day and the next morning you would both be ready for the new day's activities. You have not been passive or overly aggressive—you have merely asserted yourself in a positive, pleasant and constructive way.

WRAPPING UP

Dealing with people effectively in the changing office is becoming more complicated for several reasons. Computer technology is having a big impact. Offices are being reorganized. People are learning to adjust to the new technologies. All of this influences the ways in which people act and react to each other. You will be called on to expand your skills in dealing with the various situations and crises that inevitably arise. Meeting this challenge is very interesting and exciting and both you and your employer will benefit from your increased skill and knowledge.

3

Proven Techniques for Handling Callers

The need for skill in dealing with people is never more obvious to you than when you are acting as a receptionist. Every secretary must act as a receptionist at some time or other—even if your office employs a particular person as a receptionist. You, the secretary, always have receptionist duties. You may greet callers as they come into the office to meet with your boss, you may meet visiting dignitaries when they come to your office, you may set up meetings for your boss and greet the participants—there are numerous times in your office life when you act as a receptionist. Remember, when people come into your office they are there for a particular reason: they have an appointment to see your boss, they have come in to see a demonstration, they have stopped by for some information, they are applying for a job, they are patients to see a doctor, clients to see a lawyer, repair people to service equipment, a husband, wife, son, daughter to see a wife, husband, mother, or father. In short, they are there for a reason; they did not just wander in. Greet them with particular attention. How you handle your role as receptionist determines the mood and tone of the office. Therefore, constantly look for ways to increase your effectiveness.

SETTING THE TONE

Some of the ways in which you can increase your effectiveness are simple but easily overlooked. Take note of the following keys to success as receptionist:

1. Greet the visitor with a smile
2. Interview the visitor and get all the necessary data, such as name, firm and telephone number, and nature of business. (The information you take down depends on your boss's needs.)
3. Have visitor sign a register if this is the policy of the office.
4. Explain the procedure in a pleasant, matter of fact manner, as many busy people hate to be bothered by details such as this. Also, some people may not be familiar with this procedure. Be patient.

Remember, be particularly sensitive to visitors. Make an effort to remember the names of those who come in more than once. Clients, customers, patients—no matter who your visitors are, make them appear special. A good tip to remember is to *put yourself in the visitor's place*—for example:

> When you visit a business office for the first time, you expect to give all the pertinent information to the secretary—though it may be a bit annoying, you understand the reason for it. But if you come back a week or two later and see the same secretary, you do expect some recognition and will not like it if you are treated as if you had never been there before. You would get a feeling that this particular office does not care whether they have your business.

Now back to you as the secretary. It may be a good idea to make little notes to yourself about particular visitors, so that you are able to treat them in the best way possible. You are very busy and often cannot remember all the details that you should, but certain things are very important. People are generally sensitive about their names being misspelled or pronounced incorrectly. Once you have ascertained the correct spelling and pronunciation make note of it so that you do *not* have to ask again. If a person has a difficult name to spell or pronounce, they will be favorably impressed by the fact that you are interested enough to address them correctly.

Some clients may not appreciate being asked certain questions. If you need the information, it is good human relations to find another way to phrase the request.

For example, asking a caller whether the matter is business or personal is often a sure way to annoy him. People do not like to be put in that position. Rather, the question "May I tell Mr. Davenport what you want to discuss with him?" sounds better. Also, make certain that there is a need to ask the question at all. You may know why the caller is there. It may be at the invitation of your boss. Then it is unnecessary to get this information.

Be particularly aware while talking with the visitor of the loudness and tone of your voice. Try to speak in a low, yet distinct, well-modulated voice so that you cannot be overheard by others in the office. No one likes to feel that another, whether an employee or the president of the company, is overhearing personal business. Make sure that if anything you are discussing with the visitor is of a confidential nature, you are in an area in which you and the visitor cannot be overheard.

For instance:

> You are the secretary/assistant to the bank manager. You are very busy, the typewriter repairman is working on your typewriter, you are waiting anxiously for him to get your typewriter working again as you have a big job that must get done; your assistant is waiting at your desk for you to give her the "okay" on some work she is doing; a customer/client approaches your desk wanting to see your boss about a problem with the credit line at the bank. The customer has temporary financial difficulties. Even though you have heard this story over and over again, remember, to this customer it is of prime importance not a "run-of-the-mill" problem. It is a confidential problem, not to be overheard by others. Take special pains to talk to this person away from your desk, as the situation is too hectic there at the moment and even though *you* know that your assistant and

the typewriter repairman are neither interested nor care to listen to the customer—the customer does not know this. You will make the customer feel comfortable if you are sensitive to his feelings.

Should the visitor have to wait to see the executive, make sure that the visitor is made comfortable and from time to time indicate that it will not be much longer. No one likes to feel that they have been asked to sit down and wait and then are forgotten.

Do not carry on long personal or business conversations either on the phone or with a co-worker while you have someone waiting. This will make the person feel unimportant, uncomfortable and, sometimes, like an eavesdropper. By the same token, if you are whispering, the situation becomes even more uncomfortable because the visitor may feel that there is something being said that you *do not* want heard by the visitor.

HINTS FOR CREATING A RECEPTIVE ATMOSPHERE

Observing a visitor's appearance and actions provides important clues about the visitor, such as the seriousness or urgency of the business. Naturally, you would have asked the visitor's name and business, but by "keeping your eyes open" you may notice that a visitor is particularly nervous. Perhaps it might be a good idea to have your employer see this person as soon as possible.

Along with being sensitive to the needs of those around you, create a receptive atmosphere for visitors. The physical setup of the office is important. The receptionist should be easily visible to visitors as they enter the office. It is very disconcerting for a visitor to have to look around to see where to go. If you step away from your desk for a moment, check the reception area when you return to see if anyone came in while you were away. Do not wait for visitors to come up to you and identify themselves. It is part of your responsibility to show an interest by checking.

Remember, the customer who comes into your office and cannot find anyone is liable to become annoyed and difficult to deal with. Put yourself in the customer's place. You are a potential student visiting the office of the Dean of Students. You come into an office looking for assistance and no one is there, everyone is "out to lunch." As far as you are concerned, they may be gone forever. You do not know what to do, you may leave and the school may have lost a student. A very important key to success in dealing with people is to *always* put yourself in the place of the caller and see how you would feel if *you* were being treated by the secretary/assistant, as you, the secretary/assistant, are treating your visitors.

Now, look at it this way.

> The visitor coming into the office while you have stepped away is a very influential person, ready to give your boss a big contract. No one is there to greet the caller and your desk is piled high with a delivery from the duplication department that arrived while you were away. Nevertheless, the visitor is understanding and sits down to wait. You return and immediately get a phone call. You get very busy and forget to check and see who is waiting for your boss. By now our visitor is beginning to have second thoughts about the contract about to be awarded and approaches your desk rather angrily.

You could have avoided this problem by immediately explaining to the visitor when you returned that you are sorry about the delay but you will be right back as soon as you answer the phone. Also when you talk with the caller, make reference to the fact that the delivery from the Duplicating Department just arrived—perhaps you could say, "They are so efficient; it was a rush job and they got it to me so quickly." This will dispel the caller's fear that you are unable to keep up to date with your business. Also, apologize for not being at your desk—remember, the visitors must be made to feel important and that you care about their business.

The reception area should always give the appearance of being ready to receive visitors. Your desk should always be neat and free from clutter. The visitor who sees a sloppy desk may feel that the business is also conducted in a sloppy way.

YOUR APPEARANCE CONVEYS THE IMAGE OF THE FIRM

Your appearance is extremely important. You present the image of the firm. A grumpy or sleepy secretary will not inspire confidence in visitors. You should be well groomed, wear comfortable, yet attractive clothing, and appear alert. The type of outfit you wear (suits, dresses, skirts, or dress pants and blouses) will depend on company policy, your employer's preference, or on the image that the company wants to project. In selecting your wardrobe, choose things that are designed to give you confidence, but not to attract undue attention. Every office is different and the type of image conveyed will vary. Observe what is worn in your own office and see what image you should be conveying. In some offices such as advertising, you might want to dress a little more casually than you would in a bank or law office.

Be well groomed and pleasant looking at all times. When you are concentrating, you may tend to frown or yawn without realizing it. *Remember,* the caller who sees you yawning may feel that you are bored and not interested in either your job or the caller's business. A smile, however, makes the caller feel that you care. Your posture makes you appear alert and ready to help. It is a good idea to place a decorative wall mirror opposite your desk if possible. This is not to be used for grooming, but to keep you aware of your appearance. That way, if you are tired or concentrating on your work, you may catch a glimpse of yourself and realize how you appear to others. You may not look alert and pleasant, but rather, bored and indifferent. This mirror, if situated properly, can also reflect the reception area so that you can see if someone is getting restless.

The reason to make an attractive appearance is not to draw attention to yourself, but to add an air of confidence. This will make others—visitors and co-workers alike—feel at ease, assured that you can and will be able to handle any situation that arises.

GOOD PLANNING GETS THINGS DONE

Plan your work so that things will go smoothly. But *remember,* you cannot completely plan every step in your day. There will often be rush jobs that must be taken care of at once. Try to be flexible and accept things as they come. Do the best you can. Each office is different. In some offices, crisis situations occur more frequently than in others. If your employer is suddenly called away from the office it will affect those people who have previously scheduled appointments. They most likely will not appreciate having to prolong their waiting time or reschedule their appointments, but the way you explain and smooth things over will go a long way in allaying their disgruntled feelings. After all, any one of us could have an emergency situation at any time and it is very reassuring to know that someone is concerned enough to take the time to explain the situation and make other arrangements. For example, if a visitor has been waiting for some time and your employer is still tied up in a meeting or has not returned to the office on schedule, your duties in creating a receptive atmosphere are three-fold.

Greet this visitor cordially and be sure that your explanation of the delay is plausible, and alert your employer as soon as he is available. Another example would be:

> You are the secretary to the radiologist. A patient comes in—the x-ray machine has just broken down. Do not ask the person if he has something else to do; he probably does not, he made arrangements to be free at this time. That kind of question will only irritate him. Explain the situation, be very apologetic, suggest the alternatives—wait, come back later, and so on. But, remember, explain that what happened was totally unexpected and have the patient realize how sorry you are. Tell him that you tried to catch him before he left for the appointment. Most people will be understanding when they realize you care.

FIRST IMPRESSIONS COUNT

As already discussed, knowing your visitors is important and an easy way to help you keep up is to maintain your own personal card file on:

important clients
people frequently called
new customers
clients
potential clients

(See figures 3-1a, 1b, 1c, 1d.)

```
                                                    PROSPECT

SHERWOOD, Roselyn    (Rose' lin)
Steinman Products, Inc.
1402 Tenth Ave.
New York, NY 10023


Tel: 212-377-0707


NOTES:  Opera buff, physical fitness enthusiast, jogger
```

Figure 3-1a

```
                                                    CUSTOMER

GOLDSTEIN, Saul    (GŌLD' STEEN)  as in green
Show and Tell Computers
13-42 Circle Hwy.
Chicago, IL 44115


Tel: 312-616-7820


NOTES: Good customer of long standing; Avid football fan
```

Figure 3-1b

PROVEN TECHNIQUES FOR HANDLING CALLERS 35

If you continually mispronounce a name after you have been told how to pronounce it, or forget a name, it is a sure indication to people that you are not interested. This may not be so but that is how it appears, so you must make a special effort to remember. Perhaps in your card file or roster or on an address list, you can make notes to yourself about special things concerning visitors.

BUSINESS ASSOCIATE

First Name
CHUN, Lee Fong   (CHŪN)
Taiwan Importers, Inc.
1315 Sixteenth St.
Hoboken, NJ 08108

Tel: 201-633-5600 (Bus.)
      201-766-5020 (Home)

Notes: President of the Better Bus. Bur. of Hoboken
        Member of Board of Public Library
        Collects rare jade

Figure 3-1c

TELEPHONE NUMBERS FREQUENTLY CALLED

First Name
CHUN, Lee Fong (Miss)   Bus. 201-633-5600   Home 201-766-5020

GOLDSTEIN, Saul   312-616-7820

HARRIMAN, Esther   212-544-1678

MCINTIRE, William   212-928-0997 (Home)

MURPHY, Helen   203-129-1188

(SADOOTOE)
SEDUTTO, Anthony   914-887-1008

CAMP, James   516-438-1292

Figure 3-1d

Remember, you are the first person that the visitor sees. The impression you make is very important. The impression you make has an influence on how the visitor feels about the company. It may be a positive or a negative influence. It is very important that you make the visitor welcome. No matter how busy you are, do not appear so rushed or hurried that you give the visitors the feeling that they are imposing on you or that your employer is too busy to give them proper attention. Remember that you, in the eyes of the visitor, reflect your employer's attitude.

Put the visitors at ease. Be sensitive to their feelings. You can do this by being observant. Make the visitors feel welcome and secure in the feeling that they will be given the best possible attention by you and your employer. The key to creating this receptive atmosphere is the expression on your face—a smile and an air of calmness in the way you move. If you appear tense, you will transmit this to the caller.

AVOIDING CONFLICTS

Scheduling appointments is one of the basic but most significant operations of the office. The secretary is the most important person when it comes to arranging and setting up the daily appointment schedule. Increase your effectiveness in scheduling appointments by noting the employer's preference, and by applying some of the suggestions in this chapter.

Too often because of poor scheduling, visitors spend long periods of time waiting. The efficient secretary can learn quickly how to make effective use of the day by observing the executive's usual routine, organizing the office in the best possible way, and getting to know the customers and clients.

Often an employer makes appointments without telling you. This can present a difficult situation if you are not informed and schedule conflicting appointments. Secretaries are often faced with this situation. *You* must be innovative and find a way to deal with it.

Analyze *your* situation. If this only occurs occasionally, all that may be necessary is an apology to the visitor or client; however, if you see that it occurs frequently, then you may have to discuss the situation with your employer and come to some agreement on the best way to handle it. For example, if your employer is out of the office calling on customers all day and makes appointments without telling you, then you will have to find a solution. One way of dealing with it would be to provide your employer with a pocket calendar for noting any appointments and when your boss returns to the office, check to see if any new appointments have been made and enter them on your appointment book. Do it tactfully and pleasantly so that it is obvious that you are not annoyed but merely concerned about setting up the schedule in order to facilitate the smooth running of the office. A checklist will help you in problems like this. (See figure 3-2.)

The best approach to scheduling is to find out what your employer's preferences are and then see how you can best implement them. Approach it with the attitude that you can make it work and leave yourself open for suggestions from others. Note that every situation is different and that time allotments will vary according to needs.

Whether your employer sees visitors by specific appointment, or on a first-come, first-served basis depends on many factors such as his preference and the type of business. For example, some offices may have walk-ins while others would work only by appointment. Some people prefer a very relaxed type of office, whereas others want everything scheduled right down to the last detail.

Employers often forget appointments; people do not like to be forgotten. An otherwise calm, pleasant person may become furious if after rushing to make an appointment they find that the person they want to see is not there. It is up to you to soothe the visitor. This is not easy, especially if your boss made the appointment and not only forgot it, but also forgot to tell you about it. Certainly you cannot act as if your boss forgot. You must try to locate your boss and indicate that there was a mix-up or problem of some sort. Usually take the blame yourself. The visitor really does not get that angry at you. They are usually understanding of the situation if you apologize and try to set things right. If this situation occurs frequently, you must discuss it with your boss, but the wise thing would be to have a solution at hand—perhaps provide your boss with a note

DATE **8/6**

CHECKLIST FOR *Avoiding Conflict*

NOTES & COMMENTS *Helpful Hints Reminders*

- [x] 1. Size up the situation
- [x] 2. List the problems
- [ ] 3. List several possible solutions
- [ ] 4. Discuss with boss or bosses (tactful-pleasant)
- [ ] 5. Compromise?
- [ ] 6.
- [ ] 7.
- [ ] 8.
- [ ] 9.
- [ ] 10.

Figure 3-2

PROVEN TECHNIQUES FOR HANDLING CALLERS

pad and pencil or pocket calendar to carry and make note of appointments that come about informally while walking in the hall or in the elevator or out at lunch time (see figure 3-3 Pocket Calendar). Then you can ask your boss if there are any appointments noted. Many secretaries give their bosses a typed list of the next day's schedule each afternoon before they leave—often they remind them again in the morning (see figure 3-4 Schedule for Sept. 3). Get to know what your own boss is like. Some remember everything, others are very forgetful. Check your calendar with your boss's every day. You *have* to find a way to deal with the problem because it is one of the most common problems for secretaries. (See figure 3-5 Checklist for Handling the Forgotten Caller.)

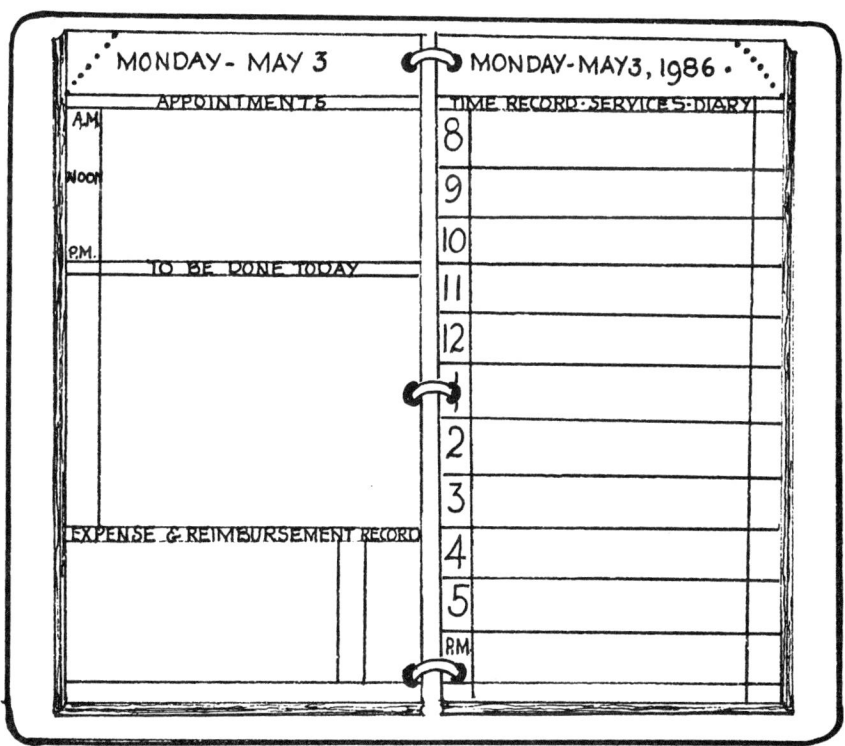

Figure 3-3

SCHEDULE FOR SEPT. 3, 19 ____

9–10 a.m.	Read mail and dictate
10–12 noon	Board Meeting
12– 2 p.m.	Lunch – Adam Simmons (Regency Grill)
2:15	Martin Jacobs – Southern Products
3– 5	Open

Figure 3-4

HANDLING PRESSURE

Even though a day may be very busy and you are extremely rushed, you must give an outward appearance of calm assurance. People must not get the impression that you are easily flustered or too busy to give them the time and attention they deserve.

Remember, everyone has concerns, whether they are personal or business related. You, as a secretary, personify the mood of the office and if you are harried or upset, if you do not feel well, if you are worried about a personal problem, you must learn not to show your concern or worry. Strangers do not think in terms of your personal problems. For example, if you have a child at home ill and you are worried about this personal problem, try not to communicate this to a customer or client. Without meaning to, you may convey the impression that you are more concerned with your own problems than with your job. As a result of your preoccupation with yourself, you might easily make mistakes and the visitor may not receive the proper attention.

PATIENCE IS BASIC TO HANDLING ALL CRISIS SITUATIONS

Keep in mind that regulating appointments carefully can enhance your employer's opportunities to expand his business. Do not become too upset should the schedule fall behind. Schedules fall behind for many reasons. For instance, in any

PROVEN TECHNIQUES FOR HANDLING CALLERS   41

DATE _9/2_

CHECKLIST FOR _Handling the_
Forgotten caller

NOTES & COMMENTS _To help me_
remember

- [ ] 1. _Apologize_
- [ ] 2. _Try to set things right (not always easy)_
- [ ] 3. _Don't blame boss_
- [ ] 4. _If happens all the time — try to solve_
- [ ] 5. _Discuss with boss?_
- [ ] 6. _Note pad and pencil?_
- [ ] 7. _Pocket Calendar?_
- [ ] 8. _Check with boss?_
- [ ] 9. _I have to find a way !!!_
- [ ] 10. _____

Figure 3-5

office it is inevitable that the unexpected may occur. Your employer may have to entertain an out-of-town business guest or an important client may have a major crisis which requires immediate attention. Such situations will occur and the alert secretary should expect them. Learn to be flexible in dealing with such circumstances—do not allow yourself to become angry or aggravated. There is no way of preventing or foreseeing these problems, so the wise secretary will adjust to the situation. Maintain an outward calm and resolve to straighten things out as soon as possible. Remember that problems can usually be resolved if only you will give them a chance.

Crises may occur in any office, but some offices are apt to have more than others. So the wise secretary will recognize this fact; and although it is not possible to schedule the unexpected, many secretaries allow "catch-up" time during the day in order to maintain an approximate schedule.

"Catch-up" time can easily be scheduled by actually scheduling "nothing" every once in a while. If your day is made up of appointments, schedule a "free" block of time at appropriate intervals. You have to examine your own situation to see how often you need this time. Timing and pacing are very important here. No one should have to wait, and if on occasion, one has to, the wait should be minimal. The "catch-up" time then should not be scheduled for the end of the day but should be interspersed throughout the day.

MAKING EVERYONE FEEL SPECIAL

Be sensitive to individual needs. *Remember*—be very careful not to dehumanize your relationships with the people in your desire to be efficient.

All sorts of situations develop in dealing with callers that require you to pay particular attention to your ability to handle people.

For example:

> A caller appears at your desk in a highly irate state. You are doing everything you should. You smile pleasantly, are willing to help, your office is neat and appears efficient, but he has arrived at your desk annoyed. Why? Unfor

tunately, the damage was done before he got to your office. Various people shuttled him from one office to another. (This has happened to all of us.) Well, all you can do in a case like this is remain calm and try to soothe and help the visitor.

This situation could have been prevented if the visitor had made an appointment ahead of time with you. You should make absolutely sure that you have given exact instructions on how to get to the building and once there how to get to your particular office.

If the visitor has come without an appointment, and this will happen often, perhaps you can make some arrangements with the reception desk or post instructions in the lobby as to the location of various offices.

Another type of situation can develop if you are in an office where security is of importance, where all your visitors must be announced. You encounter someone near your office who tells you he is looking for a particular office. You are not sure whether he actually belongs in your building, but you cannot affront or accuse him because it is possible that he accidentally walked by the security people.

What do you do? Perhaps you could offer to call someone to help him. Then call the security guards and have them go with him to the office he is looking for. You must be very careful that he does not feel accused of any wrongdoing—you may lose an important customer and a lot of good will.

The key to being sensitive to the needs of others is to imagine yourself in a similar situation. Be particularly sensitive to a visitor's feelings. For instance, when you are waiting for a train and it is delayed, you probably want to know what happened, how long is the delay going to be, should you leave the station and go to work by bus or wait longer. If you cannot find out what is happening, you may become exasperated. That is what happens to many of the people with whom you deal. There may be times when callers have to wait, but if you keep checking with them and explaining the "unexpected" situation that developed, they will feel as if you are interested.

Knowing your regular callers is very important. Some may be very impatient and not be able to tolerate waiting, others may be very happy to be offered a cup of coffee and a little conversation. Knowing individual preferences is a big help in dealing with people.

PRACTICAL TIPS FOR SCREENING VISITORS

Get as much information from visitors as possible without making them feel that they are being quizzed. Try to help the visitor yourself or at least get as much information from him as possible before going to your employer with the message. By offering to help and by getting the information, you may be able to eliminate one more call your employer has to make or another call that will require time that is not necessary. If your employer is busy or will be delayed, explain to the caller that your boss is busy at the moment and will be with him shortly. Either call on the intercom or step into the office. Make sure that the person who is waiting understands that the delay is only temporary, and that the executive will be right back. See to it that the visitor is comfortable while waiting.

Naturally, everyone has different ways of handling these situations and you must examine your own and stay by it. If you have any ideas for improving the method used, talk it over with your employer before making any change. After you have worked with an employer for a while you begin to know many of the clients or customers fairly well. However, it is wise to avoid social engagements with any of the clients, unless you make your employer aware of the relationship.

COMMON SENSE ADVICE ON HANDLING ALL TYPES OF VISITORS: SOCIAL, BUSINESS, THE VIP, SALESPEOPLE

Very often people who come into the office are from all walks of life. Be particularly careful to show no distinction in your greetings.

Your reception duties are not confined to greeting clients and customers. There will always be walk-ins such as salesmen, repairmen, delivery people, and any one of the many people who perform a service or may have reason to contact your employer. As you know, you must screen these callers carefully and treat them all with tact and courtesy. In fact, a member of your employer's family may "drop in" just when your boss has asked not to be disturbed.

The visitor who has been waiting to see your employer for some time should be informed of the delay and the reason for it. Then, ask if he would prefer to wait a little longer or reschedule his appointment for another time. Show that you want to make it as convenient as possible. If the visitor chooses to wait, offer to get a magazine or coffee or something to show your interest.

Be extra solicitous of the visitor's comfort, reassuring him often that your employer will be with him soon. Sometimes a meeting will run longer than expected and should this occur, most people will understand. Unusual situations will occur occasionally, but if they begin to happen often this is your signal as an alert secretary to analyze the situation, sit down with your employer, and discuss it to decide on the best way of handling it. There may be a number of reasons that are causing the problem. Perhaps the business is growing and gaining more clients, and the original time set aside for appointments is not enough. As you know, part of your job is to constantly be aware of situations and try to find possible solutions. Your employer has many other things to think about and may not be aware of these problems. Running an efficient office is *your* responsibility.

Remember, you must at all times be courteous and polite to callers while maintaining a warm, friendly, but impersonal relationship. This may be difficult at times.

If your employer does not schedule regular appointments, but sees visitors as they come in, you should be particularly aware of who has come in first and stick to a "first-come, first-served" schedule. If you have to deviate from this, make sure that you explain to the others waiting why someone was taken out of order. Write down their names as they arrive so that they will be seen in order. Should there be an extended waiting time, keep the callers advised with a word every now and then. Do not just seat them and go away. If you find that appointments are continually running late, perhaps you should reexamine your method of scheduling.

As you know from your own experience, there is nothing so frustrating as sitting in an office waiting to see someone, wondering how much longer you will have to wait, and then seeing someone who came in after you go in before you. You get the feeling that you have been forgotten, and if you can be forgotten in a reception area, then it is entirely possible that the business is run in a similar manner.

When dealing with people who do not speak English, be particularly careful to assure understanding on both sides. If this is only an occasional occurrence, the person can usually bring someone with him to interpret. If you are in a locality in which there are a great number of people speaking a particular language, however, it may be necessary to have someone on the staff who can speak that language. Clients who do not speak English are often fearful and do not feel confident in their ability to communicate. Remember, if you are having difficulty communicating, be particularly careful that your manner shows respect.

Elderly people require more attention than others do and you must be very patient and willing to assist. Remember, however, that elderly people are *not* children, they are *adults* and should be treated as such. Just be a little more patient and a little more willing to assist. You must be sensitive to the feelings of all but realize that certain situations have slightly different requirements on your abilities than others.

OFTEN OVERLOOKED WAYS TO INCREASE YOUR EFFECTIVENESS

Examine your situation. There may be physical aids that you can employ to increase your effectiveness. A table set up with "serve yourself" coffee can be helpful or perhaps you could have books or magazines for children if they frequently accompany their parents to your office.

Listening to yourself on a tape recorder may help you improve the tone of your voice. Speaking into a tape recorder will help you to improve your tone, voice inflection, pronunciation and enunciation, and will help minimize an accent. Some speech problems may require professional advice, and if this is the case, you should see a speech specialist.

The key to increasing your effectiveness is to be constantly aware of the importance of good reception practices and to be sensitive to the needs of everyone—visitors and co-workers alike. The responsibility for greeting visitors and getting along is a very important part of your job as secretary. Do not treat it lightly. You will be the first person the visitor sees when entering the office. The impression you make will be a reflection of your employer. Be especially sensitive to the feelings of visitors in all matters within your scope. An intelligent, poised, courteous secretary who shows kindness, friendliness, and tact to visitors and co-workers will accomplish a great deal toward creating the proper climate in any office.

CHECKLIST FOR DIPLOMACY IN HANDLING VISITORS

1. Treat each visitor as you yourself would like to be treated. Only when you realize how others feel can you treat them properly.
2. Be sensitive to individual preferences. Everyone is different and you must take this into account when dealing with people.
3. Greet the visitor with a smile. People respond to a sincere smile, because it makes them feel that you are truly interested in them. A grumpy look will cause people to respond to you the same way.
4. Achieve a positive first impression. Remember that you are often the first person that the visitor sees. You have an influence on how the visitor feels about the firm.
5. Create a receptive atmosphere. Make sure that your reception area is pleasant and neat. This will give your callers a good feeling about your firm.
6. Make an attractive appearance. If you look good you will feel sure of yourself and people will have confidence in you.
7. Plan your work wherever possible. Good planning helps things to run smoothly and people react well to a well-run, efficient office.

8. Keep an appointment book or calendar The type used will be determined by your employer's needs or preference. There are many different kinds. Analyze your needs; if you do not have the kind that suits the situation, contact or visit an office supply company or look at various catalogs of office supplies. They may have just what you want. If not, they will be able to print forms for you.
9. Record appointments carefully. Whether you use a pen or pencil is your own preference. Some people prefer pen so that the book can be a permanent record. Others prefer pencil so that they can make corrections easily. Care should be taken to spell the name correctly and the reason for the appointment should be noted. Special care should be taken not to confuse names that have a similar sound or spelling. If there is any doubt as to the name, always ask the person to spell it and then repeat it to make certain.
10. Have a telephone number where the client can be reached in case a cancellation becomes necessary.
11. Note cancellations carefully. One common method is to draw a line through the name and note when the appointment is rescheduled. This provides a record of the fact that the appointment has been rescheduled.
12. Consider the caller's preference for appointment time. If the time requested is not available, then you should offer a choice of times, for example, "Would you like to come in Friday at 3 p.m. or Tuesday at 10 a.m.?"
13. Allow time for each appointment according to the needs of the individual. You usually are able to estimate the time needed for a particular appointment or, you can say, when making the appointment, that you have a half hour free at 3 o'clock on Thursday. The caller can tell you if the time is insufficient.
14. Take care of problem situations immediately. A reason for the delay should be explained to those waiting. They will understand if they know the reason.
15. Record all appointments whether in the office or outside. Always make a note of telephone numbers where your employer can be reached at all times.
16. Note an appointment that must be cancelled in the appointment book immediately. The client or customer should be

notified and given a reason. Always treat them with courtesy and offer another appointment time.

WRAPPING UP

These guidelines will increase your effectiveness in dealing with people. But just following rules will not get the job done. You must also employ a generous amount of good judgment and common sense when dealing with people.

As the office host/hostess, it is your duty to know as much about the business as possible and to know as many of the clients and customers as possible. Know the regular customers or clients by name, pronounce their names correctly, know how to spell their names. If possible know a little about their business so that you can ask how things are and make a comment that indicates to them that you know to whom you are speaking and care about them and their business. Treat all callers with respect. You are representing the firm to your callers. Your role as office host/hostess is extremely important.

4

Communicating Effectively on the Telephone

The telephone saves time, is economical, provides rapid communication, offers convenience, and makes it possible to have information at your fingertips. Studies show that sixty percent of a secretary's time is spent communicating and a good portion of that is spent on the telephone. Almost everyone has a telephone, everyone makes and receives calls each day both at work and at home. Perhaps this is why telephone usage is taken for granted. We all think we know how to use the telephone. As children, we start using the phone almost as soon as we can talk and we continue using it throughout our lifetime, but, do we use it properly? Because the telephone is such a familiar part of our everyday lives, we do not think as often as we should about telephone etiquette.

The image you create over the telephone must be one of which your boss and your company can be proud. When prospective customers or clients call up and are answered by a bored or grumpy sounding voice they may feel the firm is not interested in their business.

Remember, when you are talking on the telephone you are not making eye contact—the image you are conveying is coming from your tone of voice, manner, choice of words, and diction.

The tone of voice or even the verbal expressions you use for social calls are not appropriate for business calls. The friendly "Hi there" or even just plain "Hello" is not appropriate for business calls. Often people mistakenly think they are setting a friendly and relaxed atmosphere, but the person on the other end of the telephone may not be concerned with being friendly or relaxed at that particular time but only interested in taking care of the business at hand as expeditiously as possible.

When you only say "Hello," the person calling has to ask "Who is this?" or, "Is this Brown Associates?" or maybe even say, "I'm sorry, I must have the wrong number." All of this wastes time and also creates an atmosphere, not of friendliness, but of inefficiency.

KEY POINTS

Three things are immediately important when answering a business phone:

1. *Identify the office and yourself:*
"Mr. Paul's office, Miss Lorenzo speaking." The caller now knows whom he has reached and to whom he is speaking. He does not have to say "Are you his secretary?" or "Who are you?"

2. *Project a positive feeling:*
"Mr. Paul is away from his office at the moment, may I help you?"
or
"Mr. Paul will return at 11 a.m., I'll have him return your call. Whom shall I say is calling?"

Do not say "Who's calling?" before indicating that Mr. Paul is not at his desk. This can give the person the feeling that Mr. Paul is there but will decide whether or not to answer the phone after he finds out who is calling.

3. *Be courteous.* Remember that the caller cannot see you. Remarks that do not seem discourteous in person may sound that way over the telephone.

For example:

> Your boss is not in and you are very busy. Several people are at your desk getting work assignments and you have just spilled your coffee. The telephone rings and you

answer it. After identifying yourself and your boss's office properly, you say, "Look, I'm very busy, I'll have to get back to you." If the caller could see the predicament you are in, he would understand—but he cannot, and this may sound very discourteous. Instead, perhaps an informative remark such as, "I'm very sorry, but we just had a little problem, may I call you back in a couple of minutes." would indicate to the caller that you care about his call, but just are unable to speak to him at that moment. Get right back to the caller as soon as you can and explain a little bit about what happened, and apologize. "Mrs. Clement, this is Miss Lorenzo from Mr. Paul's office. I'm so sorry that I couldn't speak before but my coffee had just spilled and I had to take care of it before it got on anything." Most people are understanding if they are treated courteously and are given a reason.

PRACTICING GOOD HUMAN RELATIONS ON THE TELEPHONE IS ALWAYS IMPORTANT

Today in many companies employees place and answer their own telephone calls. This saves both money and time. If the phone is answered by anyone other than the person called, the assumption would be that the person called is not available. However, often your boss wants you to screen telephone calls and tactfully determine whether the call is to be put through or not.

Always remain calm and collected, answer the telephone with a very pleasant voice, never appear hurried or harried or anxious to get to something else.

Impressions given over the phone are very important. Many people resent not being able to speak to your employer personally. In order to establish rapport with callers, handle telephone problems pleasantly, intelligently, and with confidence.

Getting more information from the caller will, of course, help you to determine what the call is about and whether your employer will want to talk with that individual now or later.

SCREENING CALLS

Screening calls is part of every secretary's job. It is a skill that requires a great deal of tact and discretion. Here are some tips to improve your skill.

1. Find out who is calling. For example, "Mr. Davenport is not available at the moment, may I ask who is calling?"

2. Find out the purpose of the call or the business of the caller. This is necessary when the caller asks for an appointment.

3. If you are familiar enough with the names of important people, you can put through those calls immediately and make decisions on whether to take a message for later call-back.

4. If you are new on the job and not yet familiar with names of callers and firms with whom your employer communicates, it is better to put through all calls at first until you become accustomed to the names and your employer's wishes.

5. The caller who wants to speak with your employer without first giving a name and the name of the company represented, should not be connected. This is what you were hired to do; therefore, you have the right to insist on this information. If the caller refuses, then politely but firmly suggest that either the caller try to contact your boss later or send a letter marked "personal."

You might say, "Mr. Davenport is in a meeting right now. If you'll send a letter marked 'personal,' I'll be glad to see that he gets it or perhaps you might like to try again later today."

PLACING CALLS

When you place calls, it is important to make sure that you are doing so correctly. Do not forget to use the call-guide page in the front of your local telephone directory, your own company directory, or your own "frequently called" list. It is a good idea to underline or highlight numbers in the directory when you look them up so that the next time they will be easier to find. The call-guide pages in the telephone directory contain all sorts of valuable information such as long distance services and call-placing methods for your particular area.

Some general tips to remember are:

1. Be sure of the number.

2. Allow it to ring long enough to give the person time to answer.

3. Be ready to talk when the person answers. If you are placing a call for your employer, be sure that your employer is ready to speak to the person being called. The person being called should not have to wait for you to call your employer to the phone.

ANSWERING CALLS FOR OTHERS

1. Emphasize names. Identify yourself and/or the person for whom you are answering.
2. Be as informative as possible.
3. Be diplomatic.
4. Be accurate in recording the name, the time of the call, telephone number, and the message.
5. If call is long distance, take down:
   a. Operator's number
   b. City and state
   c. Telephone number and extension
   d. name of caller
   e. name of company caller represents
6. If the call is long distance, remember time differences

TIPS ON HANDLING TELEPHONE CALLS: IMPROVING VOICE, DICTION, AND MANNERS

The caller must feel certain that his message will be relayed to your employer clearly. Careless taking of messages could create a major problem for the company or your employer. Your employer must be confident that you are completely trustworthy in handling the telephone.

KEY POINTS

Here are a few ideas to keep in mind:

1. Be ready with information at your fingertips or offer to find out. Anticipate objections. Time calls approximately. Have purpose clearly in mind.

2. Identify yourself and your company.

3. Find out the name and title of the person calling—"May I ask who's calling please?" or "May I have your name?"

4. Find out reason for the call—"Perhaps I can help you. What was it you wanted to discuss with Mr. Brown?"

5. Have a note pad by the telephone. (See figure 4-1.)

6. Review your notes to be certain you wrote down all the information. Do this immediately while it is fresh in your mind.

7. Confirm information by repeating or spelling names to check accuracy. Verify all numbers.

8. Allow the caller to hang up first.

Time should be used both effectively and efficiently on the telephone, but it is equally important not to rush the caller. The manner in which a problem is handled should be the major consideration of the secretary. The caller should be made to feel this through the secretary's tone of voice and attitude. Some callers do not give enough information. Here are some helpful hints on how to get the caller to talk.

KEY QUESTIONS—HOW TO GET THE CALLER TO TALK

1. Ask questions that begin with "Who, What, When, Where, Why, and How." because they require some explanation. Avoid questions that require only a "yes" or "no" such as: "Do you...?", "Are...?", "Will you...?" because they are not good conversation starters. Try questions like these: "When will the conference for magazine editors begin?", "How much longer will you be working on that project?", or "What types of equipment are you using?"

2. Ask positive questions that require an answer. For instance, "What type of advertising are you interested in?"

3. Use leading questions to obtain information like "How long have you been dealing with our company?"

4. Use open-ended questions to give you clues, such as, "What was it you found helpful in our program?"

```
To: Mr. Farley                          5/18
                                        1:30 P.M.

From: Mr. David, Reservations Clk.
      Venus Airways, Inc.

Re: Telephone Message

    Flight Info.

            N.Y. to Chicago

            May 26   FLT # 464

            LV  La Guardia  8 A.M.
            ARR Chicago O'Hare 10 A.M.


            Return Flight

            LV  O'Hare     4 P.M.
            ARR La Guardia 5:30 P.M.


                            Mary S.
```

(Figure 4-1)

5. Use reflecting phrases such as "You mentioned a new book on poetry; when will it be coming out?" or "How far along are you on your book?"

HINTS TO IMPROVE YOUR LISTENING SKILLS

The other side of the coin is that once you get the caller to talk, you must remember to *listen* to what is being said. The following hints will help you to improve your listening skills.

1. Record messages accurately.
2. Establish good rapport with the caller.
3. Ask proper questions.
4. Take good notes.
5. Anticipate what the caller will say next.
6. Flatter the caller by getting the information correctly the first time.

Remember that your voice is your only tool when you are using the telephone. It can make the difference in your ability to communicate effectively. Your voice plays a major role in the success of your employer, your company, and in your success as well.

If you are answering the telephone for more than one person, it is necessary to identify each executive by name. For example:

"Mr. Smith's office, Miss Adams speaking."

A very important rule to remember and one that is often forgotten when we are under the stress of a busy office is:

The telephone should not be allowed to ring more than once or twice, and if possible it should be picked up on the first ring.

CHECKLIST FOR IMPROVING YOUR EFFECTIVENESS ON THE TELEPHONE

When receiving a call:

1. Answer on the first ring if possible.
2. Identify yourself: "This is Miss Johnson of Smith, Smith, and Anderson."

3. Speak distinctly and loudly enough, but not too loud.
4. Be friendly and helpful.
5. Be reliable—if you promise to do something, make sure you follow through.
6. Let the caller say goodbye first.
7. If you have to be away from the phone, let the person covering the phone know <u>where</u> you are going to be and <u>when</u> you will return. If your employer leaves without telling you where he is going or when he will return, you should ask.

REMAINING CALM IS A KEY ELEMENT

If you are handling a telephone with several lines be careful when speaking to a visitor or a caller to excuse yourself and answer the telephone when it rings. As you know, it is impossible to concentrate on what you are saying while the telephone is ringing so you gain nothing by trying to finish the conversation. It is also possible that the call may be so important that every second counts. This is a very sensitive situation because each person wants your full attention. You can handle it with ease if you are calm but firm. The visitor at your desk will recognize the fact that if he were calling, he would also want to be answered immediately and not left waiting while you speak to someone else. After handling the call, thank the visitor for waiting, and resume your conversation.

PROPER HANDLING OF TELEPHONE MESSAGES

When answering the telephone, *do not say,* "Just a minute, let me get a piece of paper and a pencil." There are several things wrong with this:

1. Never answer the phone without being prepared to take a message.
2. Try not to rely on your memory.
3. Always write it down.

The rule is:

When you pick up the telephone, pick up a pencil and always have paper or message pad right there.

For taking messages, you can purchase preprinted forms or you can design your own and have them printed.(See figures 4-2a, b, c.) Take down all the necessary information. You will find the following checklist helpful. Make sure that you:

1. note the time
2. note the date
3. note the person called
4. get the name and the correct spelling. (Don't always assume your boss knows the caller or vice versa.)
5. get the telephone number—check area code and extension. People often do not indicate area code so you should ask, "Is that 212?"
6. repeat the message to make sure you have it all and that it is correct.
7. sign your name. This indicates that you are accountable for taking the message.

Let the caller know that you are writing the message down. Then repeat it to make sure you have it right. That way the caller will think, "She's good—really knows what she's doing." An extension of this is that he will have a good feeling about your company because of the impression you are communicating. Whereas, if the caller checks back later to see if your employer is in yet and you ask him to repeat the message, the feeling is, "What's wrong? Doesn't that secretary remember anything?" This can create a negative feeling toward the company.

Think about how common phrases such as "Hold on" or "I'll put you on hold" may sound. Most of us assume whenever we hear either of these expressions that we will probably never hear from the person again or we will be "lost" or "forgotten" and left on the phone. More important, what does this do to the image of your company? You may say "Hold on" and really

```
┌─────────────────────────────────┐
│ To _____ │
│ Date_____ Time_____ A.M.│
│                             P.M.│
│   WHILE YOU WERE OUT            │
│ M_____ │
│ of_____ │
│ AREA CODE & EXCHANGE _____ │
│ ┌─────────────────────────────┐ │
│ │TELEPHONED    ☐ PLEASE CALL  │ │
│ │CALLED TO SEE YOU☐WILL CALL AGAIN│
│ │WANTS TO SEE YOU ☐ URGENT    │ │
│ │RET. YOUR CALL               │ │
│ └─────────────────────────────┘ │
│      MESSAGE _____ │
│ _____ │
│ _____ │
│ _____ │
│                                 │
└─────────────────────────────────┘
```

Figure 4-2a

```
┌─────────────────────────────────┐
│ TELEPHONE MESSAGE               │
│ To:_____ │
│ _____ │
│ YOU RECEIVED A CALL FROM:       │
│ _____ │
│                                 │
│ PHONE NO._____ EXT._____    │
│ ☐ PLEASE CALL  ☐ WILL CALL AGAIN│
│ _____ │
│ _____ │
│ _____ │
│ _____ │
│ ┌──────────┬────────┬─────────┐ │
│ │TAKEN BY: │ DATE:  │ TIME:   │ │
│ └──────────┴────────┴─────────┘ │
└─────────────────────────────────┘
```

Figure 4-2b

```
┌─────────────────────────────────────────────────────┐
│  TELEPHONE CONVERSATION RECORD                      │
│  CONVERSATION WITH _____          │
│  ☐ I CALLED PARTY  ☐ PARTY CALLED ME  TIME AM/PM __ DATE __ │
│  SUBJECT DISCUSSED:_____        │
├──────────────────────┬──────────────────────────────┤
│   WHAT I SAID:       │   WHAT OTHER PARTY SAID:     │
│                      │                              │
└──────────────────────┴──────────────────────────────┘
```

Figure 4-2c

get back to the person but unfortunately, the "holder" is so used to this not happening that a negative image immediately comes to mind.

Instead of saying "Hold on," say "Wait a moment please" and then make sure it is only a moment. People who are waiting find a minute a very long time, it feels like five minutes and if they are waiting any longer than that they will probably hang up or at the very least be very irritated when you do finally get back on the line.

A good tip to remember is to give the person something to listen to while he is waiting—Music, for example, is nice. Even if he is not interested in hearing the music, he has something to occupy his mind and the waiting does not seem so long. Although many people would prefer silence, it has been found that the minute spent waiting seems much longer if the line is silent.

But *never, never* allow anyone to wait more than one minute without coming back, speaking to him, and giving him the option of either waiting or being called back. Do not ask him to call back, rather suggest that you call him.

Another tip to remember is to tell the caller what you are doing, such as "One minute please, I'll check the computer." or "One minute please, I'm on the other phone." This way the caller knows you are doing something specific and can visualize it. He does not feel that you have gone away to "parts unknown," never to return.

Also, if while talking to a person on the telephone, you have to leave the phone, explain, for example, "Please excuse me one minute, the other phone is ringing." or "Please excuse me a moment, there is an urgent delivery I must sign for." People are generally amenable to delay when they know what it is and that you are still taking care of them. After all, if your other phone is ringing or a delivery person is standing at your desk while you are trying to talk on the phone, you only have one part of your mind on either one.

People often do not hear or understand the first few words you are saying. They are so wrapped up in their own concerns that they may not focus on what you are saying. It is a good idea to get their attention by calling them by name.

Also, make sure you get the correct spelling of the name. Do not take it for granted that you know how to spell it. People may spell even the simplest of names differently than you think it should be spelled. If a person's name is Jane Eldorosio, you would ask how to spell "Eldorosio" but what about "Jane?" Couldn't that be spelled several different ways, such as, "Jayne" or "Jan" or "Jain"? Show that you care and are interested enough in the caller to get the name straight for your records so that the next time you won't have to ask. Instead you could say, "Let me see, that's Ms. Jayne (J-A-Y-N-E) Eldorosio (E-L-D-O-R-O-S-I-O) isn't it"? and the caller will think very well of you and your company.

THE PSYCHOLOGY BEHIND NAME RECOGNITION

Name recognition is psychologically important. Our names are very important to us and when someone on the telephone calls us by name, we tend to nod our head, maybe even smile in response. People always have a good feeling about being called by name and tend to pay attention to what is being said to them. A statement such as, "Mr. Johnson, this is Mary Collins. I am sorry, but Mr. Davenport will not be able to meet you for lunch today; an urgent matter came up with the data processing reports due today. He will call and explain later today."

If you had just started in with the story leaving off the names and starting with "This is Mary Collins, etc. ... ," the chances are great that Mr. Johnson may have said something like "Let me get this straight. Who exactly is this and what's the problem with Davenport?"

You see, he may not have been paying immediate attention to the first part of your story because he had his mind on other things and did not make the proper connections. This holds true even if you know the person very well. Many people feel they can save time on the phone by calling a person and immediately launching into the story. Try it sometime with someone who knows both you and the situation well and you will probably find that they ask you to repeat a part or all of what you said. The time you saved by not identifying yourself is lost while you repeat. Remember that the person answering the telephone is usually not sitting there waiting for you to call, ready to hear what you have to say.

TIPS ON DEALING WITH AN ANGRY CALLER

Always keep in mind the fact that it is easier to be annoyed and angry on the telephone than it is when looking at a person face to face. Another very important point to remember is that callers who are annoyed at something often are irate and take their anger out on you because you happen to be the first one they speak to. Perhaps the caller ordered some merchandise that came broken and has been trying to get it replaced for several weeks to no avail. He finally gets you on the telephone and is very nasty. *Do not take it personally.* This is misdirected anger. The caller is really not angry with you and you know it, but it is easy to respond the same way that you are approached and if someone is nasty to you, the tendency is to be nasty back. This can be reversed if you are calm, pleasant, and helpful. The caller will usually start to respond that way. *Do not hang up.* Be pleasant and try to calm the caller down, but *do not* actually say, "Calm down." Instead apologize on behalf of the company and indicate that you want to help resolve the problem. Reassure the caller that you will see that he gets connected to the proper person immediately, then of course, make certain the call is connected. You may have to warn the person who will take the call so that he is prepared for it and so that the caller does not have to go through the whole story again.

TAKE CONTROL OF THE SITUATION

Another key point to remember when dealing with people on the telephone is that you must learn to take command of the situation. If you speak with confidence, the caller will feel that the situation is in good hands and that you can be relied on.

Such questions as:

"How late will you be in your office?"

"Can you be reached between nine and twelve tomorrow morning?"

"Is this a 212 area code?"

are all questions that keep you in control of the situation. The following reminders will help you to maintain control.

CHECKLIST OF TELEPHONE REMINDERS

1. Pick up the telephone by the second ring.
2. Have a pencil and paper ready.
3. Say, for example, "Mr. Davenport's office, Miss Jones speaking."
4. Don't say "Hold on"; be ready to help the caller immediately.
5. Indicate that you know to whom you are speaking by repeating the name, for example, "Yes, Ms. Johnson," or "How may I help you, Ms. Johnson?"

DON'T SAY TOO MUCH

Always be aware of what you are saying when you are talking on the telephone. Often we tend to tell people more than is necessary. Even in face-to-face conversation, if the person to whom you are speaking does not respond, the tendency is to continue talking and say more and more. This is even more obvious on the telephone. A conversation might go something like this:

Secretary: "Mr. Adams office, Miss Pawling."

Caller: "Mr. Adams, please."

Secretary: "Mr. Adams is not in right now."

Caller: (Silence)

Secretary: "He probably won't be back today."

Caller: "Oh?"

Secretary: "Yes, his wife is ill."

Caller: "Oh!"

Secretary: "Yes, she might have to go to the hospital, etc., etc...."

You have moved from the professional to the nonprofessional in your manner because you have allowed yourself to be influenced by the caller's lack of response to give out more information than is called for in your conversation.

A better response would be:

Secretary: "Mr. Adams office, Miss Pawling."

Caller: "Mr. Adams please."

Secretary: "Mr. Adams is not here right now. May I have your name and I will see that he gets the message."

If the caller wants to know when Mr. Adams will return the call, you can indicate that if there is any delay, you will certainly let the caller know. Otherwise, the caller should expect to hear later today or tomorrow morning.

WHO'S MINDING THE PHONE?

Make certain that your phone is covered at all times. If you leave your desk and a call is expected, make sure you leave the message for the caller on your desk with instructions for whomever is covering your phone. When you are away from your desk, be certain that your phone is being answered properly by someone who cares and understands the importance of using proper telephone etiquette when answering and taking messages.

All your good work can go "right down the drain" when you leave for your coffee break or lunch and your phone is answered in a slovenly, uncaring manner, which is the case in some offices.

An important customer or client could be lost while you are on your coffee break because the person who answered the phone said:

> "No one's here now; they're all having coffee. Call back in 15 minutes. I don't know anything about the situation. I just happened to be passing by and picked up the phone."

You could have avoided this by making an arrangement with someone in your office to cover your phone and telling them how you want your phone answered while you are away. A simple:

> "Miss Pawling will be back in 20 minutes. May I have your name and number and she will call you back as soon as she returns."

This would avoid bad feelings.

People in your office are usually willing to help out as they all need help from time to time and will realize that it is an advantage to work together and help each other out.

We are all familiar with the Golden Rule, "Do unto others as you would have them do unto you." Well, now we can say, "Treat others on the telephone as we would like them to treat us." *Show you care*. Make an extra effort because it is easier for people to get annoyed or angry when they are talking on the phone and not making eye contact with each other.

GET HELP FROM THE EXPERTS

If you feel that the image of your company is suffering from poor telephone usage throughout the company, perhaps you can sell your boss or the personnel department on the idea

COMMUNICATING EFFECTIVELY ON THE TELEPHONE 67

of a seminar for employees on proper telephone usage. The telephone company is very helpful in this area. Contact your local representative for films and booklets. If you can get a group of employees together, you can usually arrange with the telephone company to send a representative out to your office with demonstration telephones on which role-playing will be employed to demonstrate proper telephone usage. If this is not feasible, you may want to just have a few of the booklets available to distribute to new employees.

SET UP PROCEDURES

Set up a procedures sheet for your own office on answering the telephones so that phones are covered properly and messages taken effectively even when you or someone else is away from the desk. (See figure 4-3.)

1. Whenever the executive is away from the desk, the secretary should be notified. If the secretary is away from the desk the executive should be notified.
2. If Secretary A is away from the desk, Secretary B will cover.
3. If Secretary B is away from the desk, Secretary A will cover.

(Figure 4-3)

4. If Secretary C is away from the desk, Secretary D will cover.
5. If Secretary D is away from the desk, Secretary C will cover.
6. Instructions must be left when a secretary is away from desk as to any messages expected, time of return, and so forth.

TIPS FOR IMPROVING YOUR EFFECTIVENESS ON THE TELEPHONE

Your voice becomes your personality. The image you project is even more important than your personal appearance. Follow these hints to improve your voice, diction and manner.

1. Hold the telephone properly (not too close yet not too far from your mouth).

2. Increase your effectiveness with good posture. Good posture helps your breath control.

3. Don't make the caller strain to hear you. Improve your pronunciation. Pronounce your words clearly and loudly enough to be heard easily. Make sure that names and addresses are understood. Spell names using the technique known as "key spelling." for example, "R" as in Robert, "P" as in Paul (see figure 4-4). If you know that certain words are difficult for you to pronounce, practice them and be aware of them in conversation. You can practice with a tape recorder or a friend. We often are surprised at the tone of our voice when we hear it on tape.

4. You should not smoke, eat, or chew gum while talking on the telephone.

5. Voice inflection helps to convey the meaning you are trying to get across. For example, repeat this sentence changing the emphasis each time as indicated by the underlined words.

How are you today?
How *are* you today?

How are *you* today?
How are you *today?*

6. Be careful not to talk too fast.

7. Terminology should not be too technical. Use terms that your caller understands.

8. Enthusiasm and attitude are reflected in the tone of voice, which should convey a smile. The caller will respond positively to a cheerful tone. Focus your full attention on the caller—avoid reading your mail or trying to listen to someone at your desk while you are talking on the telephone.

9. Attitude is reflected in your voice. If the day started off wrong, stop, relax for minute, and put yourself in a good frame of mind before making calls.

10. Use the caller's name. It adds importance and makes it more personal, for example:
"Good to talk with you Mr. Smith." Or "How are you, Ms. Madison?"

Use key spelling similar to the following or make up your own.

A -- Anna
B -- Bill
C -- Carol
D -- David
E -- Edward
F -- Frank
G -- Gloria
H -- Helen
I -- Ida
J -- Janice
K -- Kate
L -- Louise
M -- Mark

N -- Nancy
O -- Olivia
P -- Paul
Q -- Queenie
R -- Raymond
S -- Sam
T -- Thomas
U -- Ulysses
V -- Victor
W -- William
X -- Xavier
Y -- Yardley
Z -- Zelda

(Figure 4-4)

WRAPPING UP

Remember, in your use of the telephone you are representing not only yourself but the entire company. The telephone is an instrument of power and if used improperly, it can quickly change the image of your company from one of a caring, efficient, effective business, to one of an uncaring, disorganized, and ineffective one. You can, in a few minutes, destroy in a caller's mind the good image of your company and it is not easy to rebuild that image once it has been torn down.

5

Essentials for Improving Your Communications Skills

Dealing with people in an effective way through written communication is essential in business today. Whenever possible, you can assume much of the responsibility for composing and/or editing correspondence and other documents, such as reports. By taking over some of these tasks, you will be freeing your employer for other responsibilities and thus improving your worth.

You probably spend fifteen to twenty percent of each day handling written communications. Whether you use shorthand, transcribe from tapes or cassettes, or respond to written instructions, one of your major tasks is to turn these messages into letters, memos, and reports. You not only communicate for your boss, but also for yourself with co-workers and clients.

To assess your own communication skills, ask yourself these questions:

1. How effective are my communications?
2. Am I successful in getting the message across or getting the job done?

YOUR LETTER REFLECTS YOUR BOSS

All written documents flowing from your office reflect on your boss and the firm, and if you are involved in writing letters or composing correspondence for your boss, there are certain key points to keep in mind:

1. Be sensitive to your employer's preferences.
2. Be aware of the particular style and tone of writing.
3. Don't try to mimic exactly, but rather try to continue in a similar vein.
4. Save samples of various types of correspondence that your employer has dictated so that you can use these as a guide and speed up the task. By following these simple guides, before you know it, you will have developed a style of your own on which your boss will come to rely.

GUIDELINES FOR COMPOSING LETTERS

In any written communication, your *choice of words* is all important. Always keep in mind that what you are doing is trying to convey a message to a person. You want to have your message received and understood with as positive a feeling as possible. You do not want to affront the person by a poor choice of words. Use simple straightforward language. Imagine that you are actually speaking to the person to whom you are writing. Think about what you want to say, make a list of the points you want to include, and then write your letter. Get straight to the point. Don't lose the reader's attention or antagonize him before you have communicated the message.

Most business correspondence includes three basic elements:

1. an opening paragraph that tells what you want
2. a main paragraph or two that describe and give specific details
3. a closing paragraph that conveys a simple thank you or offers further information or help.

It is important that you end on a cordial note so that the lines of communication remain open.

Key points to emphasize in composing letters are:

1. Keep in mind the person to whom you are writing.

ESSENTIALS FOR IMPROVING COMMUNICATION SKILLS 73

2. Be sure of what you want to say (the message).
3. Verify addresses, double check dates and spelling of proper names.

<u>Remember the BASICS</u>

<u>BE</u>:
Brief
Accurate
Specific
Informative
Correct
Sincere

(Figure 5-1)

Business communications usually give information, request something, say thank you, congratulate, or offer sympathy. Make certain that all the necessary details are included. Use this simple Checklist:

1. Have you stated the purpose?
2. Who are the persons involved?
3. When do you need an answer or when does the action take place?
4. Why are you writing? Have you given the reason?
5. How is it to be done? Have you furnished all the details?
6. Where is it to take place? Furnish specific and accurate information.
7. Have you double-checked to be sure all the necessary information has been included and that all facts are accurate?

As a final check, ask yourself if you have answered these *key questions:*

Who?
What?
When?
Where?
How?
Why?

(Figure 5-2)

BE POSITIVE IN YOUR APPROACH

Use words that have a positive impact on the reader. Put yourself in the shoes of the person to whom you are writing. Think how you would feel if you had received the letter or memo you are writing. Instead of saying:

"I won't be able to attend the meeting on September 3."

say:

"I would like to attend the meeting on September 3, but will be out of town on that date. I am available anytime after September 5 or my assistant, John Parker, is available on September 3 and can act as my representative."

Leave the reader with a positive impression. Rather than flatly saying no, give the reader the opportunity to choose. Make it appear that even though you will not be able to attend that particular meeting, you want the reader to feel important and giving the opportunity to make a choice reinforces that feeling.

The following words convey a *positive* impression:

happy
opportunity

chance

pleased

and these words convey a *negative* impression:

sorry

problem

cannot

regret

Always use an appropriate closing such as:

Cordially

Sincerely

Yours very truly

Today, many offices are dispensing with the traditional salutation and closing, but the tone remains the same. The first line may be something like this:

Here is some helpful information for all homeowners.

and the closing line might be:

Call anytime on our Hotline 1-800-000-0000 for immediate assistance.

(See figure 5-3.)

IMPROVING GRAMMAR SKILLS

The best letter can lose its impact if the grammar is not correct. If there are spelling or punctuation errors, the reader will "zero in" on your errors. As you are called on to punctuate, spell, and capitalize while transcribing from dictation, editing copy on word processing equipment, or composing correspondence for your boss, you should be ready to handle this part of your work with skill.

A good handbook on English usage will aid you. If you do not already have one, you will want to get one to refer to when, for instance, a question arises about whether the period goes inside or outside the quotation mark or you are unsure about where a comma goes. The following rules of punctuation are basic to all written communication.

> **SAMPLE LETTER**
> **(Salutation and Closing omitted)**
>
> June 28, 198__
>
> Mr. Paul Fineson
> 1291 Baldwin Street
> Nashville, TN 37204
>
> SECOND REMINDER—ACG MEMBERSHIP
>
> Did you overlook your dues for the May, 198__ to May, 198__ year?
>
> If you have not already done so, please send your $35 check to ACG, P.O. Box 4962, Jackson MS 39773.
>
> We look forward to hearing from you soon, as ACG has many new and exciting plans for the coming year.
>
> MARIA T. SANTINE
> MEMBERSHIP

(Figure 5-3)

COMMA USAGE

Parenthetical words or phrases are usually set off with commas. These words or phrases, which are not necessary for the meaning of the sentence, are used to add interest or to make the sentence more readable. Examples of parenthetical words or phrases are:

> We will visit City Hall on Wednesday, or, *perhaps,* at a later date.
> I am, *however,* not pleased with the outcome.
> The repairman, *who was wearing green overalls,* entered the room.

That painting, *it seems to me,* is out of place here.

Mr. Jones, *with whom I am eating lunch,* should arrive at 10 a.m.

Introductory clauses are clauses used at the beginning of the sentence and are usually set off with commas. However, if the sentence is very short, it may not be necessary to use commas. Such clauses begin with words like:

As you may know, the firm will move to Jericho in May.

If you want further information, call 428-6590.

When the new brochure is ready, send it to all members of the community organization.

or in some cases an introductory clause begins the sentence, such as:

In case you haven't heard, Mary will return to work on September 1.

Apposition is when a word or group of words is used in reference to a person, name of a group, a company, or to describe that person, group, or company more clearly. The added explanation is usually set off with commas. For example:

Thomas Moore, *who is Personnel Director at Washington Corporation,* will be the guest speaker at the monthly meeting of the Personnel Society of Greenwood.

Dependent clauses are used to clarify the sentence and to make it more meaningful, with the result that the sentence becomes longer and slightly awkward. These clauses should be set off with commas to make the meaning of the sentence clear. For example:

Although profits for the quarter were up, the president of the company was concerned with projections for the year.

A *Compound* sentence consists of two independent clauses connected by a conjunction (and, but, or, for). An independent clause is one that can stand as a complete sentence. When there are two such clauses used in the same sentence, they must be connected in some way. This is usually done by a conjunction such as "and" preceded by a comma. For example:

Receipts for all expenses incurred on a business trip are turned over to the secretary, and she in turn fills out the appropriate expense report forms.

The conjunction may be omitted between two short clauses and a semicolon may be used instead, for example:

Susan Smith walked into the empty office; the window was open and the chair was overturned.

SPELLING AND WORD DIVISION

A good dictionary should be kept within reach at all times. You may also find it extremely helpful to keep a small 3" × 5" card taped to the desk listing the correct spelling of those words that *you* always find difficult. As a result, you will not waste time by constantly checking the spelling of the same words. (See figure 5-4)

Another trouble spot is word division.

Divide words only at syllables as the dictionary indicates, but remember certain basic rules that apply to typed copy.

1. Divide in the middle or at appropriate points:
    appoint-ment
    grati-tude
    mate-rial
2. Divide after a single letter syllable in the middle of a word:
    maxi-mum
3. Do not divide words of less then five letters, such as:
    into
    also
    ever
4. Do not divide words of one syllable.
    head
    land
    match
5. Always carry at least three letters to the next line.
    suf-fi-cient-ly (*do not* divide before *ly*)
    suffi-ciently is correct.
6. Try *not* to divide words at the end of a page.

ESSENTIALS FOR IMPROVING COMMUNICATION SKILLS

7. Divide *before* suffixes such as:
       read-*able*
8. Divide *after* prefixes such as:
       dis-figure
       con-stitute
9. A hyphenated word should be divided *only* at the point of the hyphen.
       self-addressed
       second-guess
10. Try to divide as little as possible. A letter with words divided on consecutive lines does *not* make a good impression. (See figure 5-5.)
11. Do *not* separate a single letter from the beginning of a word.
        above *not* a-bove
        erase *not* e-rase
12. If possible, do *not* divide proper names.
        Lincoln Memorial
        Thomas A. Edison

WORDS OFTEN MISSPELLED

ACCOMMODATE
ACHIEVEMENT
ACCUMULATING
ADVISABLE
*AFFECT (verb) = EFFECT (usually a noun)
ALLOTED
BENEFITED
COMMITTED
CONVENIENCE (ient)
COUNCIL (an assembly of people to give advice)
COUNSEL (advice)
DEVELOP (development)
IMPLEMENTING (put into effect)
KNOWLEDGE (Knowledgeable)
LEISURE
LIMITED
MAINTENANCE
TOTALED

* The law affected everyone.
The effect was excellent — a lowering of the rate of accidents.

(Figure 5-4)

> March 15, 198 __
>
> Mr. Joseph Vincente
> 164 Reed Avenue
> Pittsburgh, PA 15230
>
> Dear Joe:
>
> Thank you for sending the requested evaluations of the new employees.
>
> As soon as I have had time to look them over, I will include the summary in the Division Report and send you a copy along with my own personal recommendations with regard to particular individuals.
>
> Your speed in returning the reports has made my job much easier.
>
> Cordially,
>
>
> Jonathan Smith
>
> er

(Figure 5-5)

13. Divide between double consonants.
                lad-der
                set-tling

CLEAR UP THE CONFUSION OVER QUOTATION MARKS

Whether punctuation marks go inside or outside of quotation marks has always been a source of confusion. The following is helpful:

ESSENTIALS FOR IMPROVING COMMUNICATION SKILLS

1. Periods and commas *always* go *inside* quotation marks.
2. Colons and semi-colons *always* go *outside* the quotation marks.
3. Exclamation and question marks depend on usage. For example:
Mary exclaimed, "Oh my!"
        but
You're so cute, "Curly"!
Mary asked, "Did Bill go yesterday?"
        but
Is the writing "squiggly"?

MODEL LETTERS

As you know, many of the letters you write are similar. A good idea, and a timesaver as well, is to keep a looseleaf book of model letters. Check your files to see what styles and types of letters are used most frequently. Pick out several good ones or compose new ones and use these as models for recurring correspondence such as collection, thank you, inquiry, or any other type that you use frequently.

Here are some sample letters to get you started on your own personal portfolio. You will increase your effectiveness in dealing with people if you are well organized and have easy access to the appropriate letter with a minimum of changes required. Word processing equipment has made this an even more efficient process because the sample letter can be recalled, changes can be made on a video screen, and the finished product can be printed in seconds by just pressing a key.

Set up your own portfolio with a table of contents listing the various types of correspondence separated by dividers with indexing tabs. Then you can easily add or take away according to your needs. However, don't forget to constantly update as your needs change and as you make improvements. (See figures 5-6 to 5-15.)

POSITIVE LETTER

March 4, 198__

Mr. Robert D. Brown
401 Oak Street
Lansing, MI 48901

Dear Mr. Brown:

It has been some time since we have heard from you and a review of our accounts shows that your account is more than 60 days past due. You can understand that this causes us some concern.

If you have already mailed your check for $3,595 in payment, please disregard this reminder. However, if for some reason you have been delayed, we would appreciate receiving payment as soon as possible.

Should you have questions or want to discuss payment with me, don't hesitate to call.

A self-addressed envelope is enclosed for your convenience.

Thank you,

Gene Richards
er

Enclosure

(Figure 5-6)

POSITIVE LETTER
(Salutation and Closing omitted)

March 15, 198__

Mr. Robert D. Brown
401 Oak Street
Lansing, MI 48901

You are one of our valued customers, Mr. Brown.

We want to continue the good relationship we have had with you over the years. However, in order for this to happen, we would appreciate receiving immediate payment of your account in the amount of $595.

If you have been away or our previous two statements went astray, a check from you is all we need to put things right.

Our toll-free Hotline (800-100-0000) is available any weekday from 9 to 5 should you wish to talk with one of our representatives.

Thank you for your cooperation.

Timothy Smith, Treasurer
Marketing Department
er

(Figure 5-7)

COVER or TRANSMITTAL LETTER

March 10, 198__

Mr. Robert D. Brown
401 Oak Street
Lansing, MI 48901

Gentlemen:

Enclosed is the Division Sales Report for the second quarter ending, June 30, 198__.

Included in this report is the information you requested on our progress toward meeting our goals and acquiring new customers. It also shows the overall picture of growth from January through the end of the second quarter.

Should you have any questions or comments, don't hesitate to call me.

Cordially,

Jonathan Smith
er

(Figure 5-8)

COVERING LETTER

March 15, 198__

Mr. Jonathan Walsh
Jonathan Walsh, Inc.
210 Sixth Avenue
Trenton, NJ 08601

Dear Jonathan:

All facts and figures have been verified by me and my secretary, Ms. Janet Smith. I have also enclosed the Northern California report and have checked all the figures and data.

Let me know if you have any further questions and if there is anything else I can do to help you get the report out, just let me know.

When you are in San Francisco again, I hope you can have dinner with Sandy and me.

Sincerely,

Joseph P. Brown
er

Enclosures

(Figure 5-9)

INFORMATION

March 10, 198__

Mr. Joseph Vincente
164 Reed Avenue
Pittsburgh, PA 15230

Dear Joe:

For my report on sales for the Eastern Division, I have compiled data from various reports. Before writing the final draft, I need verification from you on some of the facts and figures.

On the enclosed sheets, would you check the facts and figures underscored in red to make certain they are correct before I submit the final report to the printer.

Your prompt attention to this will speed up the printing of the final copy, which we plan to get out by July 15.

I know I can count on your full cooperation, Joe.

Sincerely,

Jonathan Smith
er

Enclosures

(Figure 5-10)

ESSENTIALS FOR IMPROVING COMMUNICATION SKILLS

REQUEST

March 10, 198__

Mr. Joseph Vincente
164 Reed Avenue
Pittsburgh, PA 15230

Dear Joe:

Would you please fill out the enclosed Evaluation Reports for the four new salesmen in your division?

As soon as you can fill them in and return them, I will then be able to finish my part of the Division Report, which is due by June 30.

Thanks for always being so cooperative and prompt in responding.

Cordially,

Jonathan Smith
Marketing Division
er

Enclosures 4

(Figure 5-11)

REQUEST FOR INFORMATION

March 10, 198__

Mr. Joseph Angelo
1104 Forest Road
San Francisco, CA 94102

Dear Joe: (or instead of salutation, begin with "Joe, I need your help!")

For the year-end Sales Report for the Western Division, I need your approval to include the following before I can complete it.

        Sales for Southern California
        Sales for Los Angeles
        Sales for San Francisco

Thanks, Joe, for your help in preparing this report.

Sincerely,

(or omit closing if salutation is omitted)

Jonathan Smith
er

(Figure 5-12

THANK YOU

March 15, 198 __

Mr. Joseph Vincente
164 Reed Avenue
Pittsburgh, PA 15230

Dear Joe:

Thank you for sending the requested evaluations of the new employees.

As soon as I have had time to look them over, I will include the summary in the Division Report and send you a copy along with my own personal recommendations with regard to particular individuals.

Your speed in returning the reports has made my job much easier.

Cordially,

Jonathan Smith
er

(Figure 5-13)

> **CONGRATULATIONS**
>
> January 1, 198__
>
> Ms. Martha Rose
> 151 Sunset Boulevard
> Miami, FL 33152
>
> You're on your way up, Martha.
>
> Congratulations on your promotion to Assistant Vice President. If you don't watch out, you'll soon be running the place.
>
> I know how hard you have worked and this recognition is well deserved.
>
> My best wishes on your continued success.
>
> Janice
> er

(Figure 5-14)

Date: March 12, 198___

TO:

FROM: Jack Kelly, Chairman

SUBJECT: <u>Meeting of the Executive Committee</u>

There will be a meeting of the Executive Committee on Thursday, July 16, at 10 a.m. in the West Conference Room. We will discuss plans for the upcoming area meeting of salesmen from the Western Division. Each ad hoc comittee for planning the conference will give a progress report. All plans will be finalized.

I look forward to seeing you.

er

(Figure 5-15)

Proper Stationery Helps

Use the appropriate stationery for the type of correspondence you are sending. Your firm probably has already established a policy regarding what stationery to use for the various types of correspondence. Follow those guidelines unless you are in a situation where you are the one to set the policy and to select the appropriate stationery. If this is the case, here are some "Key Points" that will guide you in deciding what best suits your needs. (See figures 5-16 and 5-17 "Checklist of Key Points" and Worksheet for selecting stationery.)

Make a list of all these facts and decide on the type of stationery needed and the quality of paper appropriate. There are different grades of paper and you may have to do a little research on this. (See "Guidelines for Selecting Stationery" figure 5-18.) You may even make up your own forms (see figure 5-19, 5-20 Interoffice Memorandums) for interoffice memos and try them out for a while to see how they work before having anything printed.

If you are the one to set the policy for use of stationery, commercial stationers are helpful in tailoring letterheads to your needs.

You can have all the right words, but if the appearance of the letter and the quality of the paper are poor, the impression created can damage the reputation of the firm.

Stationery is like almost everything else on the market today, you can select from a wide range of quality and style, depending on the use and how much you want to spend.

It can easily be tailored to specific needs. Usually the higher quality, prestigious look is reserved for the top executives and the less expensive, general use stationery for middle managers and supervisors.

The finest quality paper is made from all cotton fiber, referred to as 100 percent rag. However, a good bond paper can be had that contains anywhere from 25 to 100 percent rag content. Stationery that would be classified as good, which might be for general correspondence, might contain from 25 to 50 percent rag content. Not only does the paper differ in quality but the printing of the letterhead would be different.

ESSENTIALS FOR IMPROVING COMMUNICATION SKILLS 93

DATE _10/8_

CHECKLIST FOR _Selecting Stationery_
Key Points

NOTES & COMMENTS _See_
"Guidelines on Selection of
Paper"

- [ ] 1. _Needs of Firm_
- [ ] 2. _Boss's Preference_
- [ ] 3. _Types of Correspondence_
- [ ] 4. _Frequency of Correspondence_
- [ ] 5. _Speed of Transaction_
- [ ] 6.
- [ ] 7.
- [ ] 8.
- [ ] 9.
- [ ] 10.

(Figure 5-16)

WORKSHEET

Needs of Firm	Boss's Preference	Types of Correspondence	Frequency	Speed of Transaction
For example:				
1. Letterhead (8½ x 11)	Best grade	Business letters	Daily—10	Reply within 10 days
2. Executive	Best grade	Personal	—3	?
3. Short & long	Sulfite	Interoffice memos	—15	Immediate

(Figure 5-17)

GUIDELINES FOR SELECTING STATIONERY

	Material	Weight	Quantity	Size	Finish	Type	Color
PRESTIGE	100% rag	24 lb	500	8½ × 11 / 7¼ × 10	regular / smooth	Bond (long grain)	ivory
GENERAL USE	25-75% rag	16-20 lb	500	8½ × 11	smooth	long grain	white
INTERNAL	sulfite	16 lb pen	500	8½ × 11	smooth	long grain	white

(Figure 5-18)

INTEROFFICE MEMORANDUM

TO: **DATE:**

FROM: **SUBJECT:**

(Figure 5-19)

ESSENTIALS FOR IMPROVING COMMUNICATION SKILLS

MEMORANDUM

TO:
FROM:
SUBJECT:
DATE:

MESSAGE: _____

REPLY: _____

Date   Signature

(Figure 5-20)

The top level executive stationery would have the "prestige" look, perhaps with raised lettering in a distinctive type style or even engraved on antique white, while the stationery for general use would look neat and crisp, bearing perhaps the company logo, name, address, and so forth, but the printing would be done by a less costly method, such as offset. For internal office use, an even less expensive sulfite (a chemical fiber) might be selected.

The chart (see figure 5-18 Guidelines for Selecting Stationery) will guide you in making decisions about what to look for when selecting stationery for your office. The chart is not meant to be complete. It is a guide to help you to know what the most important considerations are before buying.

HANDLING MAIL

A big factor in improving your ability in written communication is involved in the actual physical process of handling mail, for if a letter does not get where it is supposed to go on time the people you are dealing with will not particularly care how nice the tone is, what a wonderful grammarian you are, or how beautiful the stationery is.

Increasing your effectiveness in handling mail will save both you and your employer valuable time that can be used to good advantage in other areas. Remember to handle all mail as soon as it arrives, dividing it according to importance. You may be able to answer much of it yourself or route it to the correct person or office. Much of the correspondence you should be able to follow up on without first consulting your employer. An easy-to-follow system for processing the mail should be established and followed so that the daily handling is done with speed and efficiency.

IMPROVING YOUR PROCESSING OF INCOMING MAIL

When handling the incoming mail, keep handy a letter opener, stapler, paper clips, pencils, file folders, dater or time stamp, cellophane tape, and a mail register (a record of the date and name of the sender of all important mail received such as registered, certified, special delivery, insured, and items that contain important enclosures). This record is helpful for several reasons: (1) in case something is lost and you need to know when a piece of correspondence was received, (2) to see if all enclosures were included, and (3) because the date of receipt is important for verification.

PRACTICAL TIPS ON HANDLING THE MAIL

Sort the mail into four general groups: correspondence; bills and statements; advertisements and circulars; and periodicals and professional publications. Go through the mail and first pull out all important looking business and personal mail. Never open anything marked "personal" without permission. Put that on your boss's desk first. You may be told to open mail whether marked personal or not. In deciding on the order of importance, look at the return address. Recognizing names of the correspondents becomes routine, making it easy to determine what is most important.

HINTS ON HANDLING THE CONTENTS

Before opening the envelopes, strike the lower edge of the stack of letters on the desk to lessen the possibility of cutting the contents with the letter opener. Be sure to empty all the envelopes and attach enclosures to each letter. Check to see that the address of the sender is on the letter and, if not, attach the envelope to the letter. If a letter is not dated, the postmark date should be recorded in the register.

Each piece of mail is dated with today's date; envelopes may or may not be saved; certain things may be underlined and notations made in the margin. A letter referring to previous correspondence calls for the secretary to go to the files and pull the background correspondence referred to in the letter and attach it to the letter before giving it to the employer.

Note letters requiring follow-up or some future action in a special place such as a follow-up folder or on your calendar. Make a separate stack of those items that you can handle yourself. The following descriptions will guide you in determining the categories for sorting and rapid handling.

PERSONAL MAIL

Personal mail consists of anything other than matters directly related to the business, such as personal friends or relatives, clubs, civic organizations, and any correspondence relating to finances. The secretary should not open any of this mail unless authorized.

PROFESSIONAL MAIL

Professional mail includes any correspondence relating to the business including mail from customers, clients, professional organizations, and any writing for professional magazines, speeches, house organs, or lectures.

BILLS AND STATEMENTS

Open these after you have finished with the other mail. Follow your employer's wishes as to the procedure for handling the bills and statements. In some cases you may pay them immediately, in others your boss may prefer to take care of them.

ADVERTISEMENTS AND CIRCULARS

Go through these and add your comments to any that you feel may be of particular interest to your employer. Put those saved in a folder along with order blanks in case your employer wants to order something.

PERIODICALS AND PROFESSIONAL PUBLICATIONS

Choose the ones your employer likes to read and put them in a folder or wherever it is most convenient. Look through the table of contents noting various articles of special interest. Then you can immediately see if it is important to read the magazine now or whether it can wait until there is more free time available. If your employer happens to be writing a report, proposal, an article, or giving a talk, he will want to be up to date on everything concerning the topic.

As soon as the mail comes in, process it and arrange it on your boss's desk in order of importance with the most important on top. Sometimes, if there is an over abundance of mail at one time you may decide to save some for later, but do not make this decision unless you are positive about the importance.

CHECKLIST FOR HANDLING MAIL

1. Sort according to importance
2. Pull out important mail first and put on employer's desk immediately
3. Open and date
4. Record in mail register
5. Note letters requiring follow-up or future action on your calendar and/or tickler file
6. Separate those items you can handle yourself

WHEN THE BOSS IS AWAY

Your boss may not come into the office every day. If this is the case, read through the correspondence to:

1. determine if anything needs immediate attention.
2. write down the information from that correspondence that requires immediate action so that any questions you may have can be quickly presented when you speak with your boss.
3. acknowledge as many of the letters as possible yourself.

4. sort the correspondence and put it in labeled folders indicating that which needs attention, that which you have already acknowledged, and miscellaneous items that only have to be read.

WRAPPING UP

Your ability to communicate effectively through the written word is essential in dealing with people. When you are speaking face to face with another, certain errors in tone or grammar or wording are overlooked because you are there and it is easy to determine what you actually mean. However, in written communication the receiver must rely on what appears on the paper and if the tone is negative, the grammar poor, words misspelled, and the quality and appearance of stationery inadequate, the overall effect will be one of not caring and the image portrayed will be poor.

6

Developing Skill in Oral Communication

FIRST IMPRESSIONS ARE IMPORTANT

We identify "first impressions" often with how a person or a place "looks" to us, but what we *hear* is equally important. The "first impression" is a total feeling. If a room looks beautiful but is also so noisy that you can't hear yourself talk, then you do not care too much about it. If the furniture is nice looking but very uncomfortable, then it is not attractive to you. So it is with people, the way we look, the way we carry ourselves, the way we speak—are all a part of the initial impression that we make.

You may dress attractively, you may even write very interesting letters, so when you speak you must be able to communicate as well. We can all do this, but we may have to spend a little more time developing this skill—it is a skill and unfortunately many people do not recognize it as such.

The same person who understands the need to learn to dress appropriately, and to study to improve writing skills, often will say "I am not as articulate as Jane," and accept that without realizing that she can "learn" the skill.

And learn you must if your verbal skills are not as effective as you would like them to be. Even the sound of the voice influences the impact of a first encounter. Often we hear the phrase "a voice with a smile" because a pleasant, cheerful voice accompanied by a smile does create a positive impression.

The smile must be sincere. Many people feel that as long as they smile, they look interested, but a smile that is not sincere is often accompanied by a vacant (glazed) look in the eyes and the person to whom you are speaking is very aware that you are not really interested. Another important factor to keep in mind is the volume of your voice. It should be loud enough to be heard easily, but not so loud that it is unpleasant or grating. Tone plays a part in conveying your message, and the enunciation and rapidity with which you speak can influence how well you are understood.

It is a good idea to tape record yourself talking to find out what you sound like. Many people sound very bored or as if they just woke up when answering the telephone. They are not aware of this or they would make an effort to change. Recording your own voice in various situations and listening to how you sound often helps.

KEY FACTORS FOR EFFECTIVE COMMUNICATION

Tone of voice, pitch, appearance all influence our ability to communicate and communication in the office must include these and more. Do everything you can to keep the lines of communication open between you and your boss, your co-workers, your business associates, and your colleagues. For example:

1. Make it easy for them to talk to you. Don't act irritated or impatient when you are interrupted.
2. Respond to requests enthusiastically.
3. Be flexible so that you can drop what you are doing to take care of something else.
4. Have a sense of humor. Keep your tone light and be able to laugh once in a while.
5. Project a positive attitude about things.
6. Show a willingness to learn.

IMPROVE YOUR HUMAN RELATIONS SKILLS THROUGH ORAL COMMUNICATION

In addition to doing your job well and being a hard worker, you must get along with your boss and fellow workers. You may already possess many of the necessary interpersonal skills that will help you to get ahead in your job. You may even encounter jealous co-workers, envious of your ability and success if you use good human relations skills and are, therefore, singled out for recognition or a promotion. The way you handle such situations may have a direct bearing on whether or not you achieve the goals you have set for yourself.

Here are some tips on how you can improve your own human relations skills and your ability to communicate more effectively.

1. Treat everyone in the same friendly manner.
2. Help your boss to get ahead.
3. Be loyal.
4. Be knowledgeable about the firm and about your boss's goals.
5. Be honest.
6. Use tact, discretion, and diplomacy.
7. Avoid gossip of any kind.
8. Avoid office cliques.
9. Avoid making critical remarks about anyone.
10. Don't carry a chip on your shoulder.

Communication whether written or oral always involves three key elements. (See figure 6-1.)

1. The Sender
2. The Message
3. The Receiver

The prime goal of the sender is to have the message understood by the receiver. Often there is not a lack of communication but a lack of effective communication between two people.

Many factors influence effective communication.

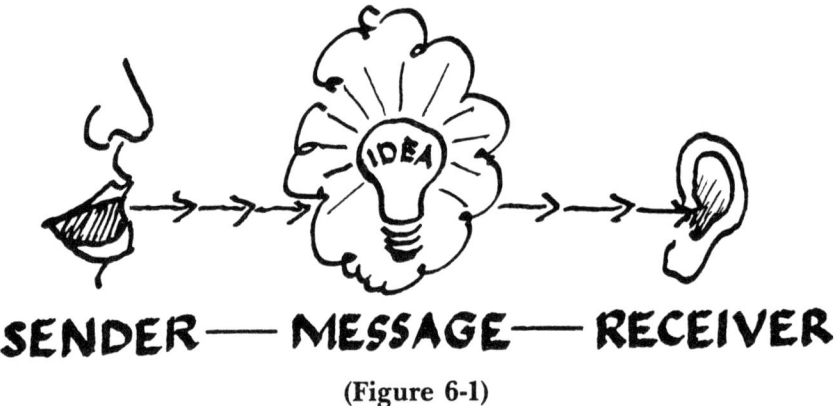

SENDER — MESSAGE — RECEIVER

(Figure 6-1)

HOW YOU SAY IT

How you say something has a great deal to do with how the message is received. Your emphasis, tone of voice, or volume conveys a message. Try to be aware of how you are coming across. Occasionally monitor yourself by observing the person with whom you are speaking to see his reaction.

Try this simple test. Repeat the sentence aloud with the emphasis on the italicized word each time and note how the meaning changes with your voice inflection.

Mr. Jones is unable to see you right now.

Mr. Jones is *unable* to see you right now.

Mr. Jones is unable to *see* you right now.

Mr. Jones in unable to see *you* right now.

Mr. Jones is unable to see you right *now*.

If your instructions are often misunderstood or people appear not to be listening when you are speaking to them, stop to analyze what you are doing wrong. Ask questions of the person with whom you are speaking to see if they understand. You might say, "Now let's check this to see if I made myself clear."

You may be conveying impatience by your tone when you actually want to communicate your satisfaction with a job well done. Remember these hints the next time you are giving instructions to a co-worker or a subordinate. Using patience and giving careful instructions will make you a more effective communicator.

LISTENING

Listening is a very important part of oral communication. If the receiver of the message is not listening effectively, even though the sender has been careful to send the message properly, it will not be received as it should be.

Listening is not passive. Listening is a skill that has to be learned and practiced because a great deal of time is spent just listening. Much critical listening takes place in the office setting listening to instructions and learning information.

The ability to hear is physical, but the skill of listening is mental and involves thinking and concentration. Your ability to be a good listener is influenced by your own personality, background, and emotions.

A good listener benefits by:

1. increased knowledge
2. broadened experience
3. further development of language skills
4. better appreciation of the spoken word
5. appreciation of sender

Inhibitors to good listening:

1. being physically tired
2. speaker's mannerisms or speech
3. noise or other distractions

TIPS FOR INCREASING YOUR LISTENING SKILLS

1. Concentrate—give your undivided attention to the speaker.
2. Do not allow outside influence or noise to distract you.
3. Interrupt and ask questions when a point is vague.

BODY LANGUAGE COMMUNICATES

The way you look and move your body sends messages, too. Your eyes and your facial expression are important communicators. Whatever the message you are trying to communicate, awareness of the way you are coming across both verbally and nonverbally is important to consider in dealing with people.

For example:

> You may be talking with a colleague while you are walking to your office. You are trying to show friendly interest in her. You may ask "How are things going?" or "Did you have a nice weekend?" She is answering you, but you can see from the way she moves that she is in a hurry and from the expression on her face that she has other things on her mind.

How do you react? More than likely you will go about your own business and forget about it, but the next time you run into her, you will probably not be so anxious to stop and talk with her. However, you should show understanding and extend a friendly greeting as if nothing had ever occurred. Chances are she had something on her mind and didn't even realize how she appeared to you. Most of us tend to make more out of something than is really there.

Posture communicates a great deal about the person speaking. It can indicate interest, lack of interest, confidence, and lack of confidence. Test yourself. Study your own expressions in a mirror or a glass window when you are talking to someone. See if you are registering the same expression on your face as you are verbally attempting to communicate, for instance, in the above example where we are trying to show "friendly interest," it may really be coming across as just that—"trying" rather than showing real sincerity.

If you really want to improve your communication skills, videotaping yourself will show you how you look and sound. So many people own video taping equipment that if you don't own one yourself, chances are you know someone who does and who would gladly tape you, talking with a client or in a mock job interview for example. This is not only a fun thing to do but the feedback is instantaneous. You can begin right away to work on those things that need improvement, such as annoying mannerisms like looking down instead of maintaining eye contact with the person to whom you are speaking. Playing with jewelry, eye glasses, or similar mannerisms detract from what you are saying. Other obvious things like slumping when you sit can have a negative effect on other people. Videotaping is an excellent way to begin to correct some of these bad habits.

Body language is composed of five areas that have a definite effect on communication.

1. *How we move our body—arms, legs, head, etc.* For example moving the head away from a speaker may indicate to the speaker a feeling of distaste.

2. *How we position ourselves in relation to others.* This is very important during meetings and conferences. If a person is sitting a little behind someone they feel left out of the meeting. A very small quiet person squeezed between two large aggressive people may also feel overpowered.

3. *How we time our verbal exchanges.* Even long periods of silence may cause a negative feeling.

4. *How we manage eye to eye contact.* If a person looks at another directly, attention is held but if the speaker looks at something other than the listener, interest is often lost because the listener does not feel the responsibility for listening.

5. *How we touch each other.* A hand on the arm or a slap on the shoulder can affect a listener either positively or negatively.

The secret of good communication is to get your message across clearly and understandably to the receiver. To do this, you must appeal to your listener by being aware of the areas that influence effective communication, for example:

1. Sender
   a. appearance
   b. style
   c. self-image
   d. background
   e. knowledge
   f. empathy

2. Receiver
    a. personal beliefs
    b. attitude
    c. physical condition
    d. emotional condition
    e. listening skills
    f. empathy
3. Environment
    a. lighting
    b. climate (hot or cold)
    c. seating arrangement
    d. noise
    e. outside influences
    f. interruptions

CHECKLIST TO IMPROVE YOUR ABILITY TO SPEAK AND DISCUSS

These simple suggestions can help you to become more effective when speaking and discussing. Mentally note the ones you are already doing and then see which ones you need to improve. It might be helpful if you made a list of the ways you can improve your speaking and discussing skills. Keep it with you at the office and glance at it occasionally as a reminder to work on those points.

1. Do you speak clearly?
2. Do you speak loud enough to be heard?
3. Does your voice convey confidence?
4. Does your voice convey a positive attitude?
5. Do you smile a lot when you are talking?
6. Do you listen attentively when someone is speaking to you?
7. Do you repeat instructions as an aid to help you remember and to check to see that you understand?
8. Do you write down instructions so that you won't forget something?
9. Do you have difficulty remembering names when introduced to someone?

10. Can you carry on small talk with a new client or with one of the executives in the firm?
11. Do you show courtesy to everyone who comes into your office?
12. Can you appear calm under pressure?
13. Are you knowledgeable about the firm?
14. Do you know the names of the important executives in the firm?
15. Are you careful not to discuss confidential business matters outside the office or even inside the office?

KEY POINTS TO REMEMBER

Your verbal communications skills will improve if you remember these key points and apply them in your job.

1. Speak distinctly and loudly enough to be understood easily.
2. Smile when you speak.
3. Be sincere.
4. Be honest.
5. Use tact, diplomacy, and discretion.
6. Treat everyone in the same friendly manner.
7. Be aware of your own body language.

WRAPPING UP

As a secretary who is constantly dealing with the public, you already recognize the importance of being understood by those with whom you are communicating. Because of the very nature of your work—taking and transmitting information of vital importance to your boss and the firm—you recognize how essential effective verbal communication is to the success of the business. As a part of a team of individuals, you can increase your skill and enhance your position as well as your boss's by following the suggestions that have been offered.

7

Here's How to Get Along with Your Bosses

You and your boss are a team—teammates must get along well together or they will not be able to accomplish the work they must do. Remember, however, that your boss is your superior. You are the assistant and it often will fall to you to be the one making the greater effort to get along.

> For example: Your boss has just returned from a business trip and work has piled up. Because he has been traveling all night and arrived just in time to come straight to the office, he is tired and grouchy. You are doing your job properly but your boss is nervous and edgy. *You* must understand this and if you are criticized or fault is found with your work, even though you know this is unfair, go along with it. Try to remain calm and do not argue. Your boss will feel better the next day and will probably apologize. Understanding the reasons for situations often makes it easier to deal with them.

It is to be hoped that your boss will also cooperate and be understanding when relating to you, but you may find yourself in the position of being the one called on to be the master in the practice of good human relations. Be ready to accept criticism, even when it is undeserved. It may come just because you overlooked something that comes under the umbrella of what is considered "the secretary's scope of responsibility."

CREATING THE PROPER ATMOSPHERE

It is important for you to recognize the broad range of duties and responsibilities your role includes. As secretary, you will have to find a way to get along with your boss or else look for another job. You cannot walk around with a chip on your shoulder saying that "He shouldn't have said that; it makes me look bad." Your role as secretary demands that you assist your boss in the work to be done, often taking a back seat and putting your boss's interests first. True, this does not give him or her the right to step on you or treat you unfairly in any way, but sometimes bosses are so wrapped up in their own affairs that they are not even aware that they are acting improperly. If this only happens occasionally or at certain high-pressure times, you should be able to let it pass. Your boss will probably apologize the next day, or, depending on the relationship you have established with your boss, you may be able to joke a little and say, "I'm glad you're in a better frame of mind today." You may even be able to say something like "I hope you're feeling more rested today, as you seemed very tired yesterday."

It is important to be aware of your own particular relationship with your boss. There is no one right answer to every situation. You have to feel your way, bearing in mind the relationship that you and your boss have.

It is interesting to note that the Professional Secretaries International defines a secretary as:

> an executive assistant who possesses a mastery of office skills, demonstrates the ability to assume responsibility without direct supervision, exercises initiative and judgment, and makes decisions within the scope of assigned authority.

The basic element here is that no matter whether the relationship is casual and friendly or strictly business, you must always keep in mind that your role as secretary is as *support* to your boss. You should not put your boss in a poor light at any time. Your first consideration should always be how your boss appears rather than how you look.

KEYS TO GETTING ALONG

Traditionally, we have thought of the boss as a man and the secretary as a woman but today that picture has changed. You can have situations where the boss is a woman and the secretary is a man, where the boss is a man and the secretary is a man, or where the boss is a woman and the secretary is a woman. Each situation brings its unique problems, but the important thing for you to remember is who *you* are. Are you the secretary or the boss? The secretary, of course—and as such you must also remember your *role*. You are there to support your boss. If you keep a clear picture in your mind of who you are and the scope and requirements of your job, you can handle any problems that arise.

MULTIPLE BOSSES

In today's automated office, having more than one boss is becoming the rule rather than the exception. This puts special pressure on you as a secretary because not only do you have to do your best to get along with one personality, you may have several different personalities to work with—each of whom operates as if you are his or her own personal secretary.

For example:

> Jean Maris is the administrative Assistant to Mary Woods, Gregory Dawson, and Phillip Prentice who are partners in Words, Words, Words, Inc., a consulting firm.
>
> Mary dictates to Jean and likes to have Jean transcribe all her letters in rough draft form so that she can revise them over and over again. Practically all the letters run more than one page. Gregory hates to dictate his own letters and just notes in the margin or on scrap paper what the replies should be and Jean composes the letter. Phillip feels that practically all letters can be made up of letters previously written so says things like "Send the same letter that we sent to Mr. Adam but use the last paragraph from the O'Doyle letter.

Jean must be a very organized but flexible person to get along with these three people all of whom have such different ways of doing things.

She keeps their work separate and deals individually with each of them, but always keeps them aware of the fact that she is working for all three. Often they all want their work in a hurry. After starting to work at Words, Words, Words, Jean soon became aware that she would have a problem if she did not come to some kind of arrangement with her principals. She noted down in a journal several typical days' activities and then requested a meeting with the three principals to work out a schedule that would help her to get all their work accomplished.

It would not be realistic to suggest that they give her the work at different times, but they have to be kept aware of the fact that there is a large volume of work and organization is necessary in order for one secretary to support all three effectively.

1. Practically all work was coming in as a "rush—must go out today."
2. Work was coming in late in day—mostly in the afternoon.
3. Each principal was operating totally independently, as if his work had preference.

After they all reviewed the journal and noted the problems presented by Jean, guidelines were established.

Jean's suggested solutions to principals were

1. Determine whether or not an order of preference was to be in effect on the work of the three principals. For example: As Mary is the President, does her work have automatic preference?
2. Principals should set priorities on the work submitted.
3. Whenever possible, work should not be submitted for same day delivery.
4. Jean should discuss priorities with principals when there is conflict.
5. Mary should use the machine to dictate. It is too time-consuming for Jean to take long dictation in shorthand.
6. Greg must be sure to be absolutely clear in the information he wants Jean to copy.

7. Phillip must be specific in reference letters so that Jean can access them without too much difficulty.
8. If Jean's office does not have a word processor, it would be very helpful to look into acquiring one. Then material could be stored, filed, and recalled, saving much time usually spent in repetitive typing.

Jean's method of handling individuals' work for herself was to:

1. be sensitive to needs of each boss
2. keep work for three principals separate
3. transcribe Mary's work in rough draft form, realize that she likes to make changes and so do not spend undue time trying to make her work perfect until she has reached the final draft
4. always check Greg's work immediately to be sure he knows what he wants, so that if Greg is not available when composing the letter it will not be a problem
5. make easy reference files on Phillip's work so that when he refers to other letters they can be found easily

It is not easy to work for several people at once, but it can be done if you keep cool and see things clearly. It is easy to get upset, but that does not help anyone. Just carefully note your problems as Jean did and find solutions to them. It is natural for bosses to think only of their own work. Often they are totally unaware of your problems, but if you present your side in a pleasant organized way showing both problems and solutions so that you will be able to give them better service, the chances are that they will be happy to go along with your suggestions.

NO STEREOTYPES PLEASE

Whether your boss is a man or a woman, you are going to have to react to him or her as a person not as a male or female stereotype. Certainly we are all different and different people react in different ways to the same situation, but, as secretaries, our first concern on the job should be getting the job done properly and this means helping our bosses with *their* work. If you are a man and your boss is a woman it is possible that you will have trouble taking orders from her. You may still see yourself as the authority figure and that may be so in your life away from your job, but on the job you must follow your job description (See figure 7-1.)

For example:

John Patterson has worked for many years as secretary to the President of the General Container Corporation, Albert Dennis. The President has retired and Dorothy Cummings, the Executive Vice President, has been appointed President.

Problem:

John is seriously considering changing his job, as he does not like to take orders from a woman. The other secretaries in the company are women, and he always felt that his position was different because he was secretary to the President.

Solution:

John has lost touch with the role of secretary. He should step back and look at his position objectively. *His* position has not changed—only his boss. With a new boss, man or woman, will come new problems because of different personalities. John, as a top level secretary, is expected to be able to deal with different personality types. He is not giving Dorothy a chance. He has a problem because he obviously sees men as authority figures and feels that it lowers his image to work for a woman.

Today we do a lot of talking about equality of the sexes, but we really must continue to be aware of the fact that problems of this nature still exist and probably will for a while. The trick is recognizing certain "hang-ups" we all have and working around them.

John needs to analyze his situation, decide whether he wants to keep his job or not and then try to get along in his new situation, realizing that the burden really is on him because *he* is the secretary—the boss's support.

JOB DESCRIPTION

TITLE ____Administrative Assist.____ JOB NUMBER _____

REPORTS TO _____ DEPARTMENT _____

RECOMMENDED GRADE _____ DATE _____

JOB SUMMARY:

Duties include handling the telephone, scheduling appointments, taking dictation, greeting visitors, organizing work, arranging meetings, delegating, and exercising initiative.

WORK PERFORMED:

Handling a busy telephone
Scheduling appointments
Taking messages
Greeting visitors
Handling the mail
Taking dictation and transcribing
Using a machine transcriber
Maintaining files
Arranging meetings
Keeping boss's calendar up-to-date
Composing correspondence
Making decisions that come within the secretary's
    scope of responsibility.

(Figure 7-1)

TEAMWORK IS ESSENTIAL

The boss-secretary relationship has been described in many ways, sometimes as a team, sometimes as a partnership. But, the basic ingredient to any teamwork or partnership is cooperation and getting along. You pull together, not separately. For you to be valuable to your boss and thus get ahead in your career, you must be the MVP (most valuable player) on the team and the boss must be the coach. This may be difficult at first but after some practice you will probably find it works.

UNDERSTANDING THE WOMAN BOSS

If you are a woman working for a woman you may encounter some other types of problems. Women have generally been more interested and involved with short-term goals rather than with the long-term or broad picture. This is, of course, because of the culture they have been brought up in and the demands that society has made on them. Today more and more women are working outside the home but women's role in the home has not changed very much. Women historically have been the homemakers and child-rearers, and as such have been responsible for the day-to-day well-being of their families. They see that they eat enough, rest enough, have clean clothes, practice proper health and personal care habits, and so forth. Men meanwhile have been the providers of the means with which the women care for the families. This built up a situation that caused women to consider goals on a short-term basis, while men were involved with long-range goals. This situation is changing, but slowly and sometimes with difficulty.

This type of orientation accounts in some measure for problems that can develop between two women working together when one is a secretary and the other a boss. Sometimes the duties and responsibilities become confused. We have to remind ourselves of the two roles. The secretary is the support person for the boss: the person who deals with correspondence; keeps the records; and handles the clerical details. The boss's role includes *creating* the work that the secretary does.

A woman boss is more apt to involve herself in a detail of the work that the secretary does. That is a basic reason why secretaries have often said they do not like to work for women—Women bosses are "picky" or "nit-picking," while men are not, "they let you do your work." The woman boss may tend to inquire more than necessary how the work is getting along or check if the secretary knows how to do it. In fact, often they are loathe to release the work and do part of it themselves. They tend to hover more over the secretary, which becomes irritating to the secretary who feels that he or she is not trusted to do the work properly.

Another reason for this situation is your boss's background—women have had to struggle to reach management or executive ranks. Most of them started where you are right now, as secretaries. Is it any wonder then that they have difficulty "turning loose" the work they once did themselves? If you can view the situation from this perspective, it might ease the situation, make your job easier, and help you to be more understanding when your boss "nit-picks."

In the last analysis, remember that you do not have the power to change people. If your boss is doing something that you do not agree with, you may have to adjust your own thinking and say to yourself, "Well, she should not have acted that way, but how can I best get along with her?"

COMPROMISE IS OFTEN NECESSARY

Often secretaries have to do things they may not be happy doing—things they may be able to accomplish better one way but have to do their bosses' way or make some kind of compromise.

For example:

> Susan Prescott is secretary/administrative assistant to Michael Trent, general manager of the Dorset Manufacturing Co. Mr. Trent holds semiannual shows of his merchandise and sends out invitations to his customers. Recently a word processor was purchased for Susan. Susan was delighted because now she could automate the mailing list and print all the envelopes. Mr. Trent absolutely refused to

have the envelopes typed. They had to be done by hand. He believed that was more personal. Susan could not get him to change his mind even after showing him how cost-effective if would be.

Finally, she realized she had to go along with what he wanted so she assigned several other secretaries the responsibility for part of the mailing list and requested them to write out envelopes whenever they had a chance so that there would always be a set of envelopes ready.

She kept the mailing list on her word processor but devised a way to earmark all changes so that just prior to the mailing it was only necessary to refer to the list and update the envelopes.

This was a compromise and even though Susan was not happy with it she had done the best she could under the circumstances because after all, Mr. Trent is the boss.

UNDERSTANDING IS THE KEY TO GETTING ALONG

A key point to remember is that understanding and being sensitive to the person with whom you are working is very important. Your gender and that of your employer do not matter—understanding is the key attribute to a successful team. For example:

> Ms. Abbott, Vice President of Sales for the Olfax Corporation was out of town at a convention of the sales representatives of personal computers in the tri-state area. She was to give a presentation on Saturday afternoon to a local community group on the advantages of personal computers for home use. On Thursday morning, Ms. Abbott discovered that she had forgotten some very important papers she needed. She immediately called her secretary, Rosa Fleming, and instructed her to send them to her. Rosa prepared the papers and took them to the company mail room with instructions that they were to go out immediately special delivery.
>
> On Saturday, Ms. Abbott called Rosa at home, "Where are the papers?" She was very upset and abusive on the telephone. Rosa got very angry and told her that she

mailed them out and nothing more could be expected of her. Rosa was so annoyed and hurt that she had a very bad weekend and went to work on Monday with her letter of resignation typed up and submitted it to the Personnel Department.

When Ms. Abbott returned from her trip on Wednesday, she was amazed to find out that Rosa had quit. She did not understand why. The copy of Rosa's letter of resignation indicated "personal differences."

What Rosa did was think only of herself. She was upset because her boss had spoken angrily to her. True, her boss should not have lashed out at her in anger without first finding out what actually took place, but on the other hand, neither should Rosa have taken it personally. What she should have done was to try to put herself in her boss's place and imagine how she would feel in a similar situation. Had she been more understanding of how her boss must have felt when it became apparent that she would have to make the presentation without the support material, she would have been able to overlook her boss's anger and go on from there. Rosa's boss was probably more upset at herself than with Rosa, but she took it out on Rosa.

Actually, if we could get behind the scene in this particular case, we would find out that Ms. Abbott was also not herself because she was very concerned about her husband. He had undergone some medical tests that were positive and he had to enter the hospital for surgery. Naturally, as she had already made the commitment to speak at this convention, she had to attend, but her mind was not wholly on it. That, in fact, was probably the reason she forgot her material in the first place. If Rosa had not been so concerned with her own personal feelings, but thought instead of her role as support to her boss, she would have remained calm and told her boss that she would see what she could do—perhaps the material had been delivered to the hotel desk and it was being held there. In retrospect, it is evident that Rosa should have called her boss on Thursday to tell her how she sent the material, and requested that the boss let her know if she did not receive it by Friday. Also, Rosa should have followed up on the mail room to make sure that the material did in fact go out exactly the way and at the time specified.

The key point to remember when handling important tasks, such as helping your boss plan for a trip or prepare a presentation, is to organize your thoughts and plan carefully step by step before you plunge into the actual work of getting things together. Make lists and check previous lists to see that everything is included. Through this process of listing and checking off, you are going through all the correct steps: (1) planning, (2) organizing, (3) following through, and (4) checking off as you complete each task.

For example, in the previous case study, Rosa thought she had done everything possible to assure that the papers would reach her boss on time. Had she used a checklist and followed up with the telephone call, she would have covered herself and reassured her boss that things had been taken care of to everyone's satisfaction.

This is a classic example that shows how misunderstandings can occur no matter how hard one tries. It is to be hoped that Rosa learned from this experience even though it was painful. The next time, she will plan better and be thorough in checking and following through.

In order to avoid the problems that Rosa encountered, the following sample checklists will help you to get your boss ready for a trip or a presentation or any major event that requires advance planning.

BASIC CHECKLIST

1. What is the preparation for: speech
    trip
    presentation
    entertaining guests
2. List everything needed and steps to take in carrying out the task.
3. Separate these things into categories and make separate lists for each category.
4. Go over this checklist with your boss to see if you omitted anything.

5. Set up folders.
6. Prioritize tasks.
7. Begin with top priority first and check off as you complete.
8. Prepare all documents, i.e., speeches, charts, reports or have them done. Check and double check each item when completed for accuracy and completeness.
9. Organize all items by labeling, etc.
10. <u>Finally</u>, check your checklist to see if anything was overlooked.

CHECKLIST TO HELP YOUR BOSS PREPARE FOR A PRESENTATION

1. Make a list of all materials needed and how many copies of each.
2. Gather all background material.
3. Find out what, if any, additional information is needed that may require several days to secure.
4. Organize this information and put it into categories in labeled folders.
5. Outline the format or main topics.
6. Begin typing any charts, statistical tables, or long reports that may be time-consuming.
7. Type up a triple-spaced rough draft from your employer's dictation or hand-written copy.
8. Retype the final presentation after it has been revised by your boss.
9. Proofread everything.
10. Double-check by ticking off [√] each item listed on your original checklist. Add any new items that were added while you were carrying out the project.

CHECKLIST ON HOW TO GET YOUR BOSS READY FOR A TRIP

1. Get the itinerary from your boss.
2. Find out what business will be transacted.
3. Find out what, if any, special papers, i.e. reports, tables, or correspondence, will be needed.

HERE'S HOW TO GET ALONG WITH YOUR BOSSES 125

4. Make a list of things to be done in order of priority, i.e. make travel arrangements first.
5. Take each item in order of priority—make travel arrangements, airline reservations, hotel reservations and ask for confirmation.
6. Gather all reports, files, etc., put them in folders and label the folders. (Make copies of originals unless originals are required, but in any case keep a copy)
7. Type up an itinerary including dates and times of departures, names of the airlines and flight numbers, arrival times in each city, names and addresses of hotels, and telephone numbers. Include a list of folders and what is in each.
8. Double check with your original checklist to see that everything has been included.
9. Follow-up on any items that have been mailed or shipped to see that they arrive at their destination on time.

If, in getting your boss ready for a trip, you fail to do something or to include some important papers, who gets blamed? You do, of course. It may not be your fault because you may not have been aware that it was needed, but the fact remains that it comes under the umbrella of the secretary's "scope of responsibility."

A good secretary becomes the boss's alter ego, and actually begins to think like the boss. If you can anticipate any needs that may develop on a trip, you can plan for such eventualities.

Getting along with your boss includes every aspect of the job. It involves give and take on both sides. Most of all, it means that you must become a master at dealing effectively with difficult situations and coming out on top.

> Maria Alvarez has just been promoted to Manager of Secretarial Services. Up until now, she had been Administrative Assistant to John Williams, Personnel Manager, but now she has a secretary of her own, Bob Franchese. Bob is new to both the business world and to the secretarial ranks, having just graduated from the local junior college with a degree in secretarial science. He could be entering this new job at a disadvantage because his boss, Maria, having been such an efficient secretary herself, may ex-

pect too much of him. Bob is going to have to learn to handle pressure well.

Some points for Bob to remember before starting the day's work are:

1. Don't take criticism personally.
2. Act professionally.
3. Take a deep breath and "look" at what he has to do today.
4. Set priorities. Make a list of what has to be done first, second, third, etc.
5. Note deadlines that must be met.
6. Evaluate—can he do all this today along with the regular tasks such as answering the telephone, greeting callers, etc.
7. Be realistic—not a martyr, but also not childish. Maria is interested in getting the job done, not in Bob's personal feelings.
8. Talk with Maria and let her know how much he can do.
9. Get to work and do the job.

Your boss depends on you to see to it that the goals of the firm are reached. This can only be done if you cooperate with your boss and help your boss to be seen in the best light by superiors, clients, and other professional contacts.

For example:

> Your boss has given you a long-report to transcribe that must be finished by the next morning, then proceeds to keep interrupting you every few minutes with other jobs that are not as important, but that will keep you from finishing the report today.

You must, of course, let your boss know you are not going to be able to finish the report. Bosses are often not aware of how much work you actually have. After a report is dictated either to a secretary or on a tape, it is off the boss's mind, but that is when you begin your work. Your boss, now that this big report is "done," starts clearing the desk of all other items. Instead of getting angry and upset, evaluate the situation, decide how much time you need and speak with your boss who probably does not even know you have a problem.

Say something like:

> "There are so many other items coming up this afternoon, I can see that I will not be able to finish the report and also take care of the other items. What do you suggest? May I assign all of the other work to one of the other secretaries, or can the report be delayed another day? I would stay and work on it this evening but I am unable to do so because of a prior commitment."

COPING WITH DIFFICULT SITUATIONS

Often your boss may do something wrong, but you have to keep reminding yourself of what your role is—you are *support* to your boss and what you are really interested in is seeing that the business of your company gets accomplished. This necessitates your boss being looked on as a competent business person. The concern is not with how *you* look, but how your boss looks.

For example:

> Your boss has an important meeting in the office with several colleagues. Some important papers needed for the meeting are missing. You, as an efficient secretary, have prepared a folder and placed it on the desk directly in front of your boss. One of the business colleagues puts some other papers on top of it. Your boss is very annoyed with not being able to find the papers, and in front of the other people, speaks curtly to you asking where the papers are.

How do you respond? Naturally you feel that you are being treated unfairly, as if you are at fault when all the time the papers are right on the desk. You feel that the other people must think you are really stupid and you do not like to look that way to them.

You could say, "There they are right in front of you where I put them." But, do you really want to do that? Your boss will look pretty bad to the others and certainly will not be happy with you for putting him in that position. Rather, you might say something like, "Just a minute, let me look. Perhaps they were misplaced." You have acted professionally, you have helped your boss, and, to the others in the room, you appear to be a very competent secretary. Whereas, in the first instance, not only have you hindered your boss, but you have also made it obvious to the others that you took the remarks *personally* and were concerned not with the employer's image and the image of the company, but with your own image.

Most business people are aware of the secretary's unique role and also aware that bosses are sometimes unfair in their approach to the secretary because they are so concerned with their own affairs. You do not hurt your image by building up your boss—you only hurt it when you forget that a key part of your job description is to support your boss. Keep reminding yourself not to take things personally and to act professionally.

BEING ASSERTIVE

Of course, you cannot allow yourself to be treated badly. Take a really good look at your situation. If you are working for someone that you really cannot get along with, even after you have practiced the best human relations possible, you may *have* to look for another position. But, before you do this, be sure that you weigh all the pros and cons—because, in most cases, you can get along with another person if you make the effort. Try to put yourself in the other person's place, try to understand him—not from your point of view—but from his.

As mentioned earlier in this chapter, employers are often so caught up in and pressured by their own problems, along with pressure from their superiors, meeting quotas, and other concerns that they overlook the fact that secretaries are human beings and not machines. You may be given too much work because your boss may not consider how long it will take you to accomplish each project. Instead of getting excited or angry, think the matter through. Calculate how long it will take you to finish these projects and then discuss the matter with your boss in a rational manner, explaining what you can do, and offer alternative solutions.

This way you have warned your boss early enough that if things continue as they are you will not be able to finish your work, but you have also given some alternatives, and exercised initiative by taking the matter into your own hands.

It is important to remember that you should *never* surprise your boss at the last minute by saying that you were unable to complete something that you were assigned. *Always* be aware of your work priorities and realize that there will be interruptions. These must be taken into consideration when planning the day's activities.

WRAPPING UP

Getting along with your boss is a big order. Keep in mind your unique role as *support* to your boss and always remember that your overall objective is to assist in carrying out the goals of your boss and firm.

8

Linking Your Employer to Others

Perhaps the most important phase of your secretarial job is that of liaison between your boss and others. *Webster's New World Dictionary of the American Language* defines liaison as:

—a linking up or connecting of the parts of a whole, as of military units, in order to bring about proper coordination of activities.

True, you have your own original thoughts that have to be transmitted to others, but your main function is of support to your boss. You may in fact be part of a larger administrative support or secretarial services department in a large firm, but you are assigned to work with and support one or more executives.

An underlying part of your role as support is that of liaison. It is not a skill that can be taught like tennis or typewriting, but it can be developed through knowledge, and awareness that the need for such a role exists. In order to be good in this role, you must have two characteristics—flexibility and adaptability. These abilities are essential because changes, compromises, adjustments will have to be made in order to achieve "the linking of various parts in order to bring about the coordination of activities."

Support means helping your bosses achieve success in their jobs. In accomplishing this, you act as liaison between your boss and all of the people with whom he or she deals. The combinations of people and situations that you are called on to handle are endless. Your skill in dealing with the situations depends on several factors—experience, knowledge, and ability to exercise good judgment. The following case studies will increase your awareness of the possible problems and will provide solutions. You will no doubt see yourself in one or more of these cases and will be able to incorporate some of the ideas presented. Your sense of awareness and your confidence in your own ability to deal successfully with such problems will be enhanced. Can you see yourself in any of the following cases?

SMOOTHING THE WAY

Madelaine is secretary to the Director of Marketing, Paula Prince. Ms. Prince is away from her office getting some information necessary for a report that Mr. Jacob Jensen, Vice President of Administration is waiting for. Mr. Jensen is anxious for the report and calls for it while Ms. Prince is away. He is quite irritated that neither she nor the report is there and wants to know why.

In this case Madelaine, in her role as liaison between her boss and her boss's superior, should respond in a positive way. Whether or not she is sure exactly what her boss is doing, she should say something to the effect that Ms. Prince was so concerned about getting the report done as quickly as possible and exactly the way Mr. Jensen wanted it that she went personally to oversee and expedite the gathering of the information. "I'll contact her and tell her you called and have her call you right back to let you know how much longer it will be."

MAKING YOUR BOSS LOOK GOOD

Bill Benton is Vice President of Sales at Universal Computer Software Company. Jacob Jensen, Vice President of Administration, is away attending a seminar concerning management decision-making skills. Before he left, he said to his secretary, Alicia Foster, "Bill wanted to attend this seminar with me and I told him I would set him up for it, but I forgot to. Call him and explain it to him. He'll probably be a little angry, so see what you can do."

Alicia did not enjoy doing this but she knew she had to. Bill and Jacob work together closely and she knew that it would create difficulty for Mr. Jensen if Bill got the wrong impression about the seminar. He might think Mr. Jensen did not want him to attend. But, on the other hand, if she simply said Mr. Jensen forgot, that would certainly give the impression that he didn't care enough about Bill being there to remember.

Alicia thought for a while about the personalities and relationships of both men and then picked up the phone and called Bill. She told Bill that Mr. Jensen thought everything was set up but discovered at the last minute that Mr. Benton had not been included. Mr. Jensen thought he had mentioned it to her. "He feels terrible and tried to get you himself but it was too early. He told me to tell you he will be in touch and to *please* forgive him. He'll make it up another time."

Then Alicia quickly made a note to contact her boss and tell him she had contacted Mr. Benton.

Alicia did not have to take the blame herself, but in this way she felt Mr. Benton might be disappointed but would probably not get angry. There are various choices that could be made in a situation such as this, but the main thing to remember is the fact that your job of secretary includes the function of *liaison and support*.

GETTING THE MESSAGE ACROSS

Mr. Jensen, Vice President of Administration, has asked you to get a breakdown of accounts receivable as of the end of last week from customers in the Southwest Division. You request this information from Don Pauling, Manager of Accounting, who wants to discuss this with Mr. Jensen before he gets the report ready. Mr. Jensen does not want to discuss anything right now. He knows Don Pauling is a very competent employee, but he also knows that Don takes every opportunity to ingratiate himself, thinking

LINKING YOUR EMPLOYER TO OTHERS 133

that this will help his career. On the contrary, it happens to irritate Mr. Jensen because he feels that it is a waste of time for both of them.

Alicia has a new problem—she has to tell Don he cannot see her boss. This situation is a little different than the one with Bill Benton because Don is a subordinate. But, in any case like this, she must still proceed with care. She must get the message across and also keep an employee happy.

Alicia thinks about it and then decides that she must be a little more direct than she was before because Don must be made to understand that the door to Mr. Jensen's office is open when their is a legitimate need but not when it is unnecessary.

She tells Don that she advised Mr. Jensen of Don's request to discuss the figures with him before preparing the report, but Mr. Jensen said that he feels it is entirely unnecessary right now and would be an inappropriate use of either of their time. As soon as the figures are prepared Don should submit them, and attach any appropriate comments that he may have. That way Mr. Jensen can review them in the light of Don's thoughts and then call him in to discuss anything if it is necessary. Alicia adds that she feels sure Mr. Jensen appreciates Don's interest.

DEVELOPING A POSITIVE ATMOSPHERE

Customers are very important to any business and all sorts of situations can occur.

A very important customer drops in to see Bill Benton, Vice President of Sales, without an appointment one day. The customer wants to see a demonstration of some new software packages that he has decided to get for distribution to a large number of educational institutions. The customer has made up his mind to buy these packages but wants one final demonstration before placing the order. Bill is away from his office at an emergency meeting because just this morning a very serious flaw was discovered in these particular software packages. The customer wants Bill's secretary to demonstrate the software as he knows she can do it.

Maria, Bill's secretary, does not know exactly how to handle this, but feels it would be inappropriate to mention the flaw until she speaks with Bill. She advises the customer that Bill was called to an unexpected meeting and that she will not be able to give the demonstration herself. However, if the customer will wait, she will see if she can locate Bill and have him talk with the customer. Either that or she will call him (the customer) as soon as Bill returns and make an appointment for a demonstration. In fact, they may be able to run over to the customer's place of business and demonstrate there to save him a trip.

The customer will probably be content because he will feel that the secretary is doing everything she can to help him even though he came in without an appointment.

Of course, in your role of liaison and support for your boss, you recognize the need to be aware of various considerations such as:

Smoothing the way for others

Avoiding conflict

Setting the scene

Developing a positive atmosphere

Supervising effectively

Handling visitors when the boss is not available

Getting people to follow the boss's instructions

Delegating authority for the boss

Making the boss look good in a difficult situation

In the case of Paula Prince, the Director of Marketing, and Madelaine, her secretary, Madelaine was smoothing the way for her boss. The report was late, the superior was irritated, and Madelaine had softened things by saying that Paula was putting forth an extra effort to see that things were done quickly and properly. In referring to the list of considerations, you can see that Madelaine was also avoiding conflict, setting the scene, developing a positive atmosphere for work, handling a visitor when her boss was not available, and making her boss look good in a difficult situation.

If you apply the same list to the situation with Bill Benton and the seminar, you will find that Alicia was smoothing the way for another, avoiding conflict, setting the scene, developing a positive atmosphere, and making her boss look good in a difficult situation.

In the situation with Jacob Jensen and Don Pauling, you can identify the following considerations:

Smoothing the way for others

Avoiding conflict

Setting the scene

Developing a positive atmosphere for work

Getting people to follow the boss's instructions

Delegating authority for the boss

Supervising effectively

Bill Benton's secretary, when handling the important customer also was:

Smoothing the way for others

Avoiding conflict

Setting the scene

SHOWING RESPECT

Care must always be taken to give the proper respect to all people. In particular, however, those who are our superiors in the business setting must receive the respect due their positions. This is especially true in front of clients, customers, and other outsiders or the liaison role will not be successful. After working closely with someone for any period of time, it is easy to lose track of the fact that they hold a superior position and deserve the respect due that position.

For example:

> You and your boss are on first name basis. Your boss is hosting a meeting with some very important clients. You enter the meeting and say, "Is there anything else you would like me to do, Joe?" After the meeting your boss

expresses his annoyance that you called him by his first name during the meeting.

You think this is very unfair, and maybe it is, but, as a top notch secretary/administrative assistant, you should have realized that in front of others you should address your boss more formally. The scene being set is one of business-like formality, not social informality, and clients should not be aware of anything other than a well-run, efficient organization able to care for their needs.

TIPS FOR SUCCESSFUL LIAISON WITH THOSE YOU SUPERVISE

As a secretary, you may supervise other employees such as typists or junior secretaries who assist you. Always be sure that you do supervise these people. There is a big difference between the people who are directly under your supervision and those whom your boss supervises but to whom you carry your boss's instructions.

When you supervise other employees, make sure they understand what they are doing. Often a part-time typist or junior stenographer really has no understanding of the job and feels that you, the secretary, are just "throwing your work off" on him or her. Always make sure that the people you supervise understand the nature of the work they are doing, and praise them for jobs well done. Be aware of and sensitive to their needs. If it is necessary to criticize their work, try not to do so in front of others. The following checklist will provide you with some guidelines.

CHECKLIST FOR SUPERVISING OTHER EMPLOYEES

1. Give clear, complete instructions
2. Make sure they are understood
3. Make certain that the person doing the work is aware of the nature and importance of the job
4. Be sensitive to the person's needs
5. Be honest and direct

6. Praise work whenever possible
7. Use tact in criticizing work
8. Request assistance rather than issuing orders
9. Make each employee aware that his contribution is just as valuable as anyone else's
10. Don't forget to say thank you

Carrying instructions to your co-workers from your boss can be a very sensitive area. If you are not careful how you present the instructions, these workers may resent you and feel that you are not just passing on instructions, but "ordering them" to do something on your own. On the other hand, if you are not assertive enough, they may not carry out the instructions.

You are on a tightrope—you *must* get the job done as your boss expects you to—so you need to be very sensitive and aware of how you are coming across to your co-workers.

How you communicate to others is very important and so many factors are involved (see Chapter 6). The following Checklist will be an aid to you.

CHECKLIST FOR OVERCOMING BARRIERS TO COMMUNICATION

1. Find a common ground of understanding (put yourself in the other person's place)
2. Choose the most opportune time
3. Communicate face to face
4. Observe how the message is received
5. Use immediate feedback to reinforce message (voice, facial expression, and body movement)

Motivation is very important in your role as liaison for your employer. If you must supervise people for your employer, you need to be sure that they are interested in doing the job assigned. Generally speaking, a person does not do a good job if he has little interest in it. Your job is to see that the job is done well for your employer.

The following tips may be helpful in motivating your co-workers.

CHECKLIST ON HOW TO MOTIVATE THE PEOPLE YOU SUPERVISE

1. Diversify the work (variety).
2. Allow them the freedom to make some decisions on their own.
3. Schedule work hours as flexibly as possible.
4. Involve co-workers in the decision-making process.
5. Set clearly defined, realistic goals.
6. Give co-workers an opportunity to be creative—suggestion boxes, recognition for ideas to improve the way things are being done.
7. Compliment co-workers—let them know they are appreciated and needed.
8. Show your support to co-workers, especially in front of others.
9. Use job descriptions that are goal oriented.
10. Help co-workers achieve personal goals that are in keeping with those of the company.
11. Be a good listener.
12. Do not ignore or forget your co-workers.

DEVELOPING A POSITIVE ATMOSPHERE

No office can function properly if it is not maintained physically. Getting along with the maintenance people in your organization is very important.

> For instance, you arrive one morning and find that the air conditioning system is not working and the office is very warm. Your boss has a group of VIPs coming in to look at his operation. You call maintenance and tell them your problem. You must be careful how you approach them, because they are people and have feelings, and even though you are furious with this disruption in your well-laid plans, you should not let this show. After all, you want them to help you. What is to be gained by yelling at them. Tell them the terrible predicament you are in. Explain that as secretary you are responsible for the physical setup of

this meeting and now *you* are in big trouble. Can the maintenance people help you out?

You will probably find that an approach like this will get more results than reprimands.

YOUR ROLE AS LIAISON WITH OTHERS

It seems to be a very easy task, in fact, not even a task at all. After all, you are only linking your boss with others—carrying your boss's instructions or messages to others. But this may not be as easy as it seems. Sometimes, the instructions or messages you have to carry are distasteful to the receiver. Because the person cannot express his feelings to your employer he will take them out on you.

For example:

> Jeannette Fried is secretary to Mr. Jeffrey Ollander, Vice President of Marketing for the Happy Face Frozen Dessert Company. A customer, Mrs. Jones, calls demanding to speak to Mr. Ollander because she had ordered a large quantity of Frozen dessert for a party she was hostessing for a local political candidate for the state senate, and it was all spoiled. You know about this problem because your boss has had other complaints. The refrigeration in a truck transporting the frozen dessert to that area had broken down and the driver was not aware of it until much later that day when he was making another delivery and found that the frozen desserts had all melted and were spilled all over the truck. He immediately reported it but it was too late to do anything about the earlier deliveries.
>
> Your boss does not want to deal with any of the complaints. In fact, he has told you that "there are not going to be many happy faces from that area of the state." He said, "Tell them we are sorry and that we will replace the desserts, but whatever you do don't put them in contact with me. I do not want to talk to any of them."

Naturally, Mrs. Jones, the customer, has been severely embarrassed and needs to yell at someone. She is a very important customer and in a position to influence other customers. You should remain calm, offer apologies and deliver the message but do not get angry. Be professional—keep in mind that Mrs. Jones is not really angry with you, but with the situation. Make her aware of the fact that your boss will be advised personally of her situation and is very concerned.

If you lose patience with her, you are not acting as liaison for your boss, but rather alienating your boss and the customer and causing serious problems for the firm. It is important to be aware of where your role as liaison begins and ends. It is very easy to take on your boss's job without realizing that you are doing so. In the above situation, Jeannette's boss gave her full authority to deal with complaining customers. He had confidence that she would do the right thing. Even though he told her he did not want to be in contact with any of them, Jeannette had to make her boss aware of this situation. After she had spoken with Mrs. Jones, she should have written a note to Mr. Ollander advising him of the situation and suggesting that he may want to speak with or write to Mrs. Jones personally.

One of the biggest complaints among customers, clients, or business associates is that they "can't get past the secretary to see the boss."

This is all well and good, but to be really valuable in linking your boss to others, you as secretary need to continually evaluate and reevaluate the situation, keeping in mind this often overlooked but perhaps most important aspect of your job.

WRAPPING UP

You, as a secretary, can think of hundreds of situations in your everyday office life where you act as liaison and support for your boss. The following checklists will be invaluable aids to increasing your effectiveness in this area.

CHECKLIST FOR DEVELOPING A POSITIVE ATMOSPHERE

1. Look on the bright side, be an optimist.
2. Display a sunny disposition—smile and be pleasant.
3. Keep your personal problems separate from the office.

LINKING YOUR EMPLOYER TO OTHERS 141

4. Listen to what others have to say.
5. Encourage ideas and suggestions from co-workers.
6. Delegate work and give individuals the freedom to handle it without interference.
7. Encourage and promote cooperation among co-workers.
8. Help the negative individual to look at the positive side by asking the appropriate questions.
9. Turn negative situations into positive ones.

CHECKLIST FOR THE SECRETARY AS LIAISON FOR THE BOSS

1. Support your boss.
2. Be understanding.
3. Show initiative.
4. Be perceptive.
5. Never underestimate your boss.
6. Listen to what is said without interrupting.
7. Make certain that those concerned know what it is you are trying to accomplish (communicate effectively).
8. Admit your mistakes.
9. Don't assume anything.
10. Be willing to rectify mistakes.
11. Be positive.
12. Be loyal.
13. Be helpful.
14. Use tact and diplomacy.
15. Do not repeat rumors.
16. Keep everything that occurs in the office confidential.
17. Coordinate.
18. Possess a clear understanding of your duties.
19. Be flexible.
20. Cooperate.

9

Increasing Your Effectiveness as a Supervisor

One of the secretary's many duties is the role of office supervisor. The secretary's responsibilities with regard to running the operation of an office depend on several factors. The job can be challenging, involving many different activities.

Depending on the size of the staff and the levels of employees included, you as secretary/supervisor will allot an appropriate percentage of your time to duties that involve supervision. Your role is expanded because you not only have to get along with your boss but also with the staff. You often are responsible for the smooth running of the office. The secretary who is willing and able to assume the job of office supervisor becomes a valuable asset to the firm.

In a small office you may actually be designated the "office manager" and be directly supervising the other employees. In a larger office you may be supervising the employees indirectly by seeing that your boss's orders are carried through. In other situations you may indirectly be supervising the entire office and directly supervising people who report to you—such as assistants, junior secretaries, word processing or corresponding secretaries, filing or clerical people, and office temporaries.

Whatever your particular duties as supervisor are, you must get along with the people you supervise and get them to work *for* you; otherwise you will be ineffective as a supervisor.

MOTIVATING YOUR STAFF

Always remember that your aim as a supervisor is *not* showing your power, but rather, getting the job done. If you approach your supervisory functions as a method to show the "power" you have, you will probably get poor results. The aim is to get the job done and to motivate your people to be interested enough in what they are doing to do the job.

One of the main problems in many job situations that keep the job from getting done is that some employees do not understand the importance of what they are doing. Every job is important. Even the most menial or seemingly unimportant job, if it is not done properly, can have a bad effect on the final outcome of the entire project.

The important thing to remember is that everyone needs to understand their particular job and feel a sense of pride and importance in doing it well. This is one of the most important principles to remember when trying to motivate people.

People must also be equipped to do the job assigned. Motivation will not help if the person does not have the background, ability, or necessary equipment or support to do a job. So, choose your people and your assignments carefully. If a job needs to be researched, make sure the person you assign to it knows how to research and has the background material available to do the research. If the job requires composing from researched material, see to it that you either choose someone who already knows how or train people to do this. Do not give people assignments that they are not able to handle without giving them the training and support to help them. No matter how motivated a person is to do a job, if he does not know how, he will not be able to do it properly.

JOB DESCRIPTIONS ARE HELPFUL

One of the first steps in supervision is to delineate duties for jobs. If the firm does not already have job description sheets, it is a good idea to prepare a job description for each of the positions in your office. This will help to clarify what each person does to aid both the worker and the supervisor. All the duties of a particular position should be listed and possibly name the immediate supervisor. If your firm has job descriptions on file, it is important to keep them under review to see that they reflect current duties. Remember, the people who actually do the job should be consulted when updating job descriptions because people often take on tasks that are not reflected in the description.

In fact, it is important for you, as secretary/supervisor, to remember to keep a list of your own duties current because many of your duties, including your supervisory functions, may not be on *your* job description. (See figure 9-1.)

If you do not have standard forms in your office, you can make up your own (see figure 9-2).

JOB DESCRIPTION

NAME:
JOB TITLE: Secretary/Administrative Assistant
ABBREVIATED JOB DESCRIPTION: Perform all the secretarial and administrative duties required as support to the Vice President of Marketing and colleagues.
DUTIES:
    Scheduling appointments
    Organizing and maintaining files and records
    Setting up travel itineraries
    Making travel reservations
    Screening phone calls
    Arranging meetings and conferences
    Researching background material for reports, speeches, and articles.
    Compiling reports
    Typing and transcribing dictation
COMMUNICATION SKILLS:
    Dealing with customers and clients, and fellow workers
    Using proper telephone techniques
    Editing—Use of good grammar and spelling

Figure 9-1

INCREASING YOUR EFFECTIVENESS AS A SUPERVISOR

```
JOB DESCRIPTION
Name _____

Job Title _____

Training _____

Duties _____
_____
_____
_____
_____
_____
_____
_____
_____
_____

Date _____ Signature _____
```

Figure 9-2

LINES OF AUTHORITY

Depending on the size of the office, it may or may not be necessary to designate the lines of authority. (See figure 9-3.) For instance, the secretary who is also the office manager would report directly to the person in charge. The part-time clerical help or the custodial staff would report to the secretary/office supervisor.

There are few jobs that are as diversified as secretary/office supervisor. Duties for this job include being a receptionist, secretary, bookkeeper, clerk, and assistant. Being the office supervisor as well as secretary may add on many more duties, such as scheduling and assigning work; giving instructions; seeing that the work is done on schedule; being a human relations expert in maintaining good relationships among the office staff; and scheduling vacations and days off.

As mentioned before, the extent of the supervisory function depends on several things—the size of the office, the type of office, the number of other secretaries working, and the degree to which your employer is willing to relinquish the role of manager and delegate it to you. Because executives are generally more involved in administrative functions related to their work, the trend is to allow the secretary more responsibility in the area of office management.

In your expanded role as office supervisor, you may no longer be personally responsible for preparing certain letters or reports, but it is still your responsibility to see that they are done correctly. Therefore, the secretary as an office supervisor/manager has the responsibility to delegate some duties to others and see that they are done properly. Your responsibility may extend to checking up on the custodial staff to see that their jobs are being done properly; assigning vacations to the various members of the staff; arranging for coverage while they are away; preparing the payroll; seeing that equipment is maintained properly and repaired when necessary; keeping an inventory; ordering office supplies and equipment; and acting as a liaison between your employer, the staff under your supervision, and other professional associates.

For example, an organization chart showing the lines of authority in a typical office might look like the following.

Analyze your own situation. Make an organization chart similar to the one following. Examine your own situation to see if the lines of authority are clear. Are there certain gray areas where it is not clear who reports to whom? Suppose you have written a proposal for the purchase of new equipment, but you are not clear about how you should proceed with gaining approval.

As secretary/supervisor you must be very sensitive to the amount of authority delegated to you by your manager. Your first step would normally be to get your boss's approval before

INCREASING YOUR EFFECTIVENESS AS A SUPERVISOR 147

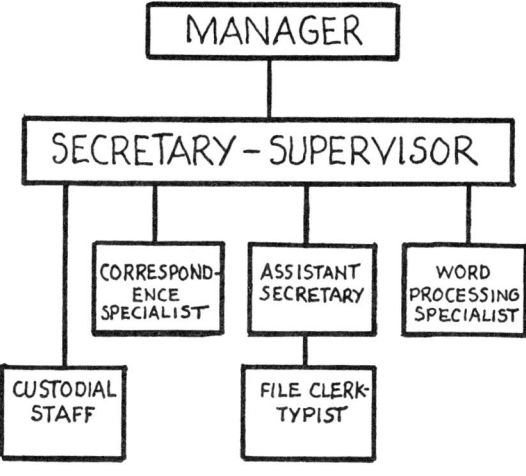

Figure 9-3

starting to write a proposal, but your boss may have delegated this authority to you and therefore you would get his approval after you have written it. These are the "gray areas" that you must clear up after analyzing your situation.

In many instances temporary or part-time people must have the duties of their positions explained. The secretary may have to schedule the working hours of the various employees so that they will be on hand when needed by the firm.

THEORIES OF MANAGEMENT

If your job requires supervisory or management duties, you should acquaint yourself with the various styles of leadership. If you have never studied management theory, now may be the time to take a course to help you become more effective as a supervisor. Although much of dealing with people is founded on common sense, we should be as well versed in the fundamentals as possible. The most common leadership styles are:

Dictatorial leader—This type of boss expects employees to do well or they will suffer the consequences. The employees' morale is generally not good. This approach usually can only be effective for a short time.

Paternalistic leader—generally benevolent; subordinates depend on the leader for all decisions. If leader is not around, employees do not do well. They also generally do not develop into leaders themselves.

Laissez-faire leader—does not really want to be responsible. Everything is delegated and subordinates often work on their own, making their own decisions, and setting their own goals. This can result in confusion.

Democratic leader—Everyone participates in all goal setting, planning, organizing, and decision making. A sense of cooperation is felt, but sometimes the process of accomplishment is long.[1]

Generally a supervisor or manager practices a combination of styles. There are times when you can be the democratic leader and have everyone cooperate on planning and times when you must be the dictatorial leader and tell your subordinates exactly what to do. There are situations where it is better for your subordinates to depend totally on you and other situations when they can be totally responsible for making their own decisions.

For example:

Mary Lou is supervisor of the Word Processing Center. She assigns all work to her employees and sets all rules and regulations regarding formatting of material and time limits for submission. She holds weekly meetings of her staff and encourages open discussion of the problems that they encounter and their solutions. All employees in her department are entitled to a three-week vacation but no more than two employees may take vacations at the same time. Employees are encouraged to work out their vacation time with each other. Mary Lou appoints her assistant to oversee the arrangements.

Mary Lou practices all four leadership styles depending on the circumstances.

---

[1] Howell, William C. and Dipboye, Robert L., *Essentials of Industrial and Organizational Psychology*, The Dorsey Press, 1982, pp. 136-140.

INCREASING YOUR EFFECTIVENESS AS A SUPERVISOR

You should be familiar with common theories of management such as Douglas McGregor's Theory X and Theory Y,[2] which are briefly stated below.

> *Theory X*—states that people do not like to work, avoid it as much as possible, get no satisfaction from it, have very little originality and ambition, and need to be directed in order for business goals to be achieved.
>
> *Theory Y*—is the opposite to Theory X, stating that people like to work, are self-directed, do not need control or threats of punishment, are rewarded by ego satisfaction, will seek responsibility and creativity, and their intellectual potential is generally underutilized.

ACHIEVING GOOD INTERPERSONAL RELATIONSHIPS WITH YOUR ASSISTANTS

Getting along with your assistants is very important. In order for people to do a good job they must feel happy about what they are doing and achieve a sense of job satisfaction. This will largely be up to you as supervisor. You have to set the tone in the office. Your staff must work with you, not against you. To do this, they must feel that you are fair with them and that you have the knowledge to be in a supervisory position.

You must set down certain guidelines that are basic to achieving good interpersonal relationships with your assistants.

Your assistants are there to *assist* you. You have the authority to be their *boss*. There must be no question of this authority. There cannot be an informal relationship. Your authority must be clear. Often in an office a secretary is asked by her boss to assume certain authority without the lines being clear.

For example:

> Moira's employer, the Vice President in charge of Sales, asked her to be responsible for the planning and setting up of a special seminar for their salesmen in the Southwest

---

[2]McGregor, Douglas, *The Human Side of Enterprise,* McGraw-Hill Book Company, Inc., 1960, pp. 33-57.

division. This required the enlisting of the aid of many of the office staff including sales managers, secretaries, clerks, and typists, along with the Reprographics Department and so forth. When Moira approached the people, they were willing to help. They did not however consider the project a priority job, but one that they would do after they got their other work done.

Also, the Reprographics Department would not accept any work on Moira's authority, but needed it approved by her employer. All of this was a problem because immediately after appointing Moira to this project, Mr. Daley, the Vice President of Sales, went on vacation for three weeks.

Of course Moira should have asked her boss to issue a memorandum to all involved informing them that Moira was in charge of this project and asking them to put it as a top priority item and cooperate. Then there would have been no problem.

The principles are clear:

1. *People must be informed.* Even if Moira practiced all the rules of good human relations, she would not have succeeded in this project if the others did not cooperate. They probably would not cooperate if they did not feel that she had the authority to take over this project.

2. *Your assistants must be aware that you have the knowledge to do a job.* A supervisor does not have to be an "expert" in each phase of a particular job, but must be an "expert" supervisor. Your assistants are there to be the experts in the various areas assigned, but you must have the overall knowledge to tackle the job and properly oversee it. Your assistants must recognize your ability.

3. *You must be fair and understanding when dealing with people.* When a job is assigned, the person must understand the job in relation to the entire project and must be given the proper amount of time and physical backup necessary to accomplish it. For example: if the job requires a lot of phone calls, the person must have a phone easily available. If the job requires work after hours, the person must be given overtime or compensatory time and this must be explained at the outset of the assignment. Above all, your assistants must feel free to come to you and discuss the project with you.

4. *You must set clear time limits or deadlines.* Be fair in your time limits. Do not want it "yesterday"; allow a reasonable amount of time and be firm in your time limits. People very quickly learn that "she wants it Wednesday, but that probably means she will wait until Friday." Set *realistic* time limits and goals—something that can be accomplished. It is devastating to a person to try to accomplish something that is impossible.

5. *Be willing to praise people for a job well done, but be sincere in your praise.* Insincerity is very obvious to people and you do not gain the respect of the people you supervise if you are insincere.

6. *Never reprimand a worker in the presence of another.* If you feel that you must reprimand someone, do it in private. The other workers should not be privy to this. Also, before you reprimand someone make sure you are not at fault. Perhaps you have been unrealistic or unfair in what you have asked or not provided the proper support and backup. Even if you are right in what you expect, it is usually better to "discuss" the situation with the assistant rather than reprimand him. Sometimes people are not sure what is really expected of them.

7. *Keep in touch with the job you are supervising.* Do not just assign and leave. Ask people how they are doing, do they need any help. Perhaps require progress reports. This way everyone knows you are still interested and they are not forgotten in what they are doing. Also, by your keeping on top of the job, you are less likely to have problems—the situations will be caught and resolved before they become problems.

PROVIDING A GOOD WORKING ATMOSPHERE

As a supervisor, you should be aware of other factors that could influence the people you are supervising. The physical conditions under which the people work have a great deal of effect on them. Anything you can do to make the office more attractive and more comfortable for those working, as well as for visitors, is an asset.

The furniture and equipment used in the office should be adequate for the tasks performed. Sometimes a job is not being done because the person is uncomfortable at the particular work station and so is not turning out enough or the proper work.

> Jessica works on a word processor all day, with two 15-minute coffee breaks and an hour lunch. There is only one word processor in her department and she handles the work for seven lawyers. There are four other secretaries who take dictation and type but all lengthy material goes to Jessica. She should be able to handle the work but finds that her eyes and her back bother her so much that she is getting slower and slower. She has checked with her doctor but there is nothing physically wrong with her. Finally it occurs to her that the problem must be working at the machine.
>
> Susan, the secretary/supervisor, has been concerned about Jessica's slowdown. When she hears about the backache and eyestrain, she remembers reading about these problems in an article on word processing. She calls the manufacturer and asks them to send someone in to talk with her. It is determined that the lighting and furniture are not proper for the equipment. Also, Susan remembers that she has heard that people should not be on the machine as long as Jessica is. Of course, it is not feasible to keep the machine idle so Susan decides to suggest to her employer a system of cross training so that another one of the secretaries can learn the machine, and share the job with Jessica. This was tried and proved successful. So, in combination with rearranging the location of the work station, getting better lighting and a more ergonomically effective table and chair, and by cross training and job sharing, Jessica no longer was suffering eyestrain and backache and the work output was back to normal.

TIME MANAGEMENT

Careful planning is of key importance in managing your time more effectively. Think in terms of long-range goals and then decide how best to achieve them. Once you begin the process of setting goals, one of the first steps is to make a checklist or set up a schedule in the form of a worksheet to help you organize the tasks into a workable plan. By doing this, you will be able to pace yourself, accomplish the most important things first, and eliminate or postpone those tasks that can wait. Be aware of when you are most productive and schedule those jobs that require the most concentration for that time. Leave other less demanding tasks for another time. Don't try to be a perfectionist. Just be realistic and do the best that you can. Trying to handle too many jobs under pressure of a deadline can slow you down or block progress altogether. Rather than allowing this to happen, try keeping a log of your activities all day long for a week or two. Then analyze it to see what tasks you can eliminate, delegate, or combine. Then rank them according to priority. You will have a much clearer picture of how your time is spent and what you can do to improve your handling of it.

As suggested by Lauren Januz and Susan Jones in *Time Management for Executives*,[3] become a list and schedule maker and keep a calendar. Plan your activities for the month. On your desk, keep an up-to-date tickler file, and as you complete each day's tasks, place the index guide in the back of the file.

If you supervise other employees, you may run into a situation where office morale is low and output slows down. No matter how capable people are, unless their efforts are recognized and rewarded by the one in charge, loss of interest and poor results will begin to show. When people know that what they do is important to you and to the goals of the firm, they will want to do good work and help out in whatever way they can to meet the goals of the firm. People like to know that what they do is significant, that they are an important part of a team effort. Most people want more responsibility and greater challenges.

SETTING PRIORITIES

Setting priorities is important in any situation. Dealing with a variety of people in an office setting brings into play

---

[3]Januz, Lauren Robert and Jones, Susan K., *Time Management for Executives*, Sidgwick & Jackson, 1981.

many different personality types and backgrounds. Unless there are certain established guidelines to follow, things may not get done efficiently and may, in fact, deteriorate to such a point that total confusion results. The idea is not to allow this to happen. Keep ahead of the game by setting standards and following certain priorities in dealing with people.

CHECKLIST FOR SETTING PRIORITIES

1. What are the goals of my firm?
2. What are the top priorities set by my boss?
3. Do they fall in line with those held by the firm?
4. What are my responsibilities as spelled out by my job description?
5. Which tasks contribute the most toward achieving the goals of my firm and my boss?

INCREASE YOUR EFFICIENCY WITH CHECKLISTS

Develop a routine to be followed to see that the office is ready each day. This could be set up in a checklist showing the various duties broken down into weekly, daily, and periodic tasks for which you are responsible. This would be an aid to you because sometimes even though these duties become automatic, in a busy office they can easily be overlooked if you find yourself interrupted by several emergencies just as you are about to do something. With checklists already made up, the tasks could be delegated to someone else. Checklists offer several advantages:

1. serve as an organizer and goal setting tool
2. set priorities
3. help to orient new employees or temporary workers
4. save time spent explaining
5. increase efficiency of the office

CHECKLIST OF SECRETARIAL DUTIES

Open mail and distribute
Bring boss's calendar up to date

INCREASING YOUR EFFECTIVENESS AS A SUPERVISOR

Bring your calendar in line with boss's
Record any new reminders on calendar
Check tickler file and bring up to date
Check pending file
Get ready for instructions from boss and/or to take dictation
Transcribe dictation
Type and send out any routine correspondence
Maintain schedule of recurring bills, payments, insurance premiums, professional dues, periodical subscription renewals, rent, loan payments, etc.
See that recordkeeping is up to date
Keep files current
Keep vacation schedules, sick leave, and personal days up to date
Handle billing if applicable

CHECKLIST OF SUPPLIES AND EQUIPMENT

Check office equipment to see that it is in good working order—typewriters, word processors, transcribing machines, telex, telephones, computers, etc.
Call service people when needed
Check inventory of office supplies to see what needs to be replenished or reordered
Make out supplies requisition or order
Dispose of outdated supplies

CHECKLIST OF SERVICES

Arrange for maintenance and repair of equipment
Check on cleaning of office
Check on florist who takes care of plants
Call exterminator when needed

CHECKLIST OF HOUSEKEEPING DUTIES

Check room temperature
Check air freshness
Check reception area for neatness, chairs, and sofas in order, periodicals neatly arranged
Check ashtrays
Turn calendars to current date
Set clocks if needed
Check plants—water and dust
Check windows, mirrors, floors, and carpets
Check boss's office

WRAPPING UP

Remember that as secretary/office supervisor, you often have the responsibility of managing the office staff. The degree and scope of your responsibility is determined by the size of the office staff and the policies set by the firm. A smooth-running office depends on workers who do their jobs properly and although your role as office supervisor may be tedious and exacting at times, it is always challenging.

KEY FACTORS FOR SUCCESS AS A SUPERVISOR

1. Know your employees—their strengths and weaknesses.
2. Allow time for employees to adapt to your style.
3. Be flexible.
4. Challenge employees with responsible assignments.
5. Be creative—vary from the expected.
6. Give clear, complete explanations.
7. Be supportive.
8. Respond to employees' needs and desires.
9. Be sincere, honest, and fair.
10. Learn how to delegate—to whom and what.
11. Move slowly in making changes.
12. Be on lookout for potential trouble spots.

Whether at home or in the office, learn to manage your time so that you can utilize every moment to the fullest. Skillful time management allows you to accomplish everything you are supposed to do and have time left over for other pursuits either related to your job or for personal enjoyment.

10

Focusing on the Public

The importance of human relations in any office is obvious when we think of the constant personal contact between the secretary and the boss, co-workers, clients, business associates, and other members of the office staff.

Human relations include the many ways that people interact with each other. In the field of human relations, people concentrate on finding better means of getting along with each other both individually and collectively. The study of human relations is based on the idea that every individual has the right to be treated with dignity and respect.

In an ever-changing, fast-moving, competitive society such as ours, the need for building good human relations is increasingly important. Where there is more competition, there is naturally more pressure put on the secretary and executive to be the very best in their field and to make sure that the public knows this. Your employer and his staff must project a good image.

Every individual has the right to be treated as you would expect to be treated yourself. In short, practice the golden rule: "Do unto others as you would have them do unto you."

PROJECT AN ATTITUDE OF CONCERNED GRACIOUSNESS

The secretary plays a major role in establishing good relationships with the public. This relationship has a definite effect on the reputation of both the employer and the firm, whether it be a small community, town, or city. Although the secretary is not the only one responsible for building good relations, it is a vital part of the job and having the right personality for the job can be very important.

For example:

> Carla Montega is a legal secretary. An irate client calls her law firm looking for a particular lawyer. The lawyer is not available but the client is so disturbed over some injustice that he feels has been done him that he verbally abuses Carla. She in turn is so annoyed with him that she responds by telling him that he should not speak to her this way, it is not her fault.

Carla is not practicing good human relations here. She should have tried to calm the client down by saying something like, "Mr. Pauling, I am terribly sorry you have this situation. Let me locate Steve Frederickson, who should be able to help you. Where can I reach you? I'll call you right back."

By using this approach, Carla is projecting an attitude of concerned graciousness. This is indicated by a willingness and ability to help and by not taking the client's verbal abuses personally. This action was professional on the part of the secretary. It is not a matter of whether it was the right way for the client to treat the secretary, but rather how you as secretary handle the situation.

The secretary should be prepared for and expect to deal with a certain amount of verbal abuse and rudeness from clients. The secretary is usually the first contact that anyone has with the boss or with the company; therefore, the secretary unintentionally becomes the target of pent-up anger.

Being able to deal with people in a pleasant, tactful way, both face to face and over the telephone, is a quality that is absolutely necessary for the secretary.

For example:

> A client has been trying to get the executive on the telephone for hours and because of some mix-up with the answering service, the message did not get to the executive.

You as secretary should not be influenced in your responses by the actions of others. In this instance, rudeness on the part of a client requires that you respond with tact and politeness. A common mistake is that people say, "I would be nice to him, but he did not treat me right." After all, it is not the fault of the client. This would be a test of your ability to practice good human relations. First, calm the client and then deal with the attitude by suggesting that perhaps he should be willing to excuse such an error this time. If you use a positive approach, the individual will usually respond accordingly.

Because you are human, there will be times when it will be difficult to practice good human relations. It may be that today is not your best day: you have a headache; there are some family problems that must be resolved; or you are waiting anxiously for news of the results of your brother's surgery. Because you are a secretary, you cannot allow this to influence the way you deal with others. The important thing to remember in building good human relationships with people is that a person can only direct his or her *own* actions; and in so doing, act in a manner that reflects good will for the executive and the company.

EVEN-TEMPERED BEHAVIOR SPREADS GOOD WILL

In an executive-secretary-client relationship, it is important that the client feel comfortable and wish to continue the relationship. The secretary plays a major role in building and maintaining such an ongoing relationship.

One way to foster such a relationship is to call people by name. Coming into a pleasant, cheery office and being greeted by a secretary who shows genuine interest can change a person's whole attitude. Always remember to smile and say something pleasant, such as "Good morning! May I help you." Your own office and the type of people with whom you deal will determine the length of time spent on pleasantries. You may be in a very busy office dealing with people who are always in a hurry—they may not want to chat about the weather. On the other hand you could be in a doctor's office where a patient wants to chat a few minutes.

You have to be particularly sensitive to your office situation. Examine the type of people with whom you deal—do not make up one formula and apply it to all. People are all different, but, generally, all respond to being treated pleasantly and with respect.

TIPS ON GREETING VISITORS TO YOUR OFFICE

A visitor likes to feel that the executive and the secretary care and are interested. It is important that you demonstrate a sincere, active, and concerned interest in the visitor's comfort. You as the secretary can help the executive in building this feeling by reminding the executive what the caller's business is. For example:

> "Mr. Johnstone from the Environmental Center is here to see you. He is chairing a committee of local residents who are terribly worried about the fact that the digging at the 56th Avenue site may injure the roots of trees that border it. Here is the file on that job."

This may be a very volatile situation and anything that can be done to show that your company has the interest of the community in mind will be helpful. Just the fact that your boss knows about the problem and will be able to greet the caller with a word or two such as "Good morning, Joe! Let's see what we can find out about the situation. We wouldn't want to lose those beautiful trees." would set a positive tone to the meeting.

Otherwise, when Mr. Johnstone comes in and your boss is not aware of the situation, he may just say "What can I do for you?" and then find out he has a big problem on his hands without having had time to do any research at all. Valuable time will be lost in rebuilding a relationship that would not have suffered if the secretary had prepared the boss.

In a busy office, with a full schedule ahead, there is always the temptation to cut corners, but, no matter how you feel about it, the caller feels that the reason for the call is important. Exchanging a few words with each caller, giving him a warm smile, extending a cordial greeting, or saying an unhurried goodbye will go a long way toward both building and improving the image of your firm. Use the following checklist of hints as a daily reminder of the key points to emphasize in your contact with the public.

HINTS FOR DEALING WITH THE PUBLIC

1. Greet each caller cordially.
2. Show a genuine interest.
3. Treat everyone with equal respect.
4. Stop and think before you speak.
5. Respond with tact and politeness.
6. Be consistent.
7. Call people by name whenever possible.
8. Leave a good impression with an unhurried good bye.

TIPS ON DEALING WITH THE UNEXPECTED

It is a good idea to have the telephone numbers of your employer's colleagues or business associates available should your employer be called away suddenly or have to go out of town. A caller must always feel confident that he will be able to contact the executive if the need arises. This is part of the continuity that the client must feel—that the executive has a personal interest and that his problems are an ongoing concern of the executive.

It is a part of your responsibility to guard against client dissatisfaction with any services, fees, or other aspects of professional services. Dissatisfaction can result in complaints that will undermine the confidence of the people who do business with your firm. Even though most complaints are unjustified or stem from misunderstandings, their existence can create serious problems.

You are familiar with the old saying "foresight is better than hindsight." Much can be learned from the mistakes of others, *if* we heed this advice. In a sense, this is what education is all about, being forewarned about possible areas that can create problems. There are many areas in any office where problems can be avoided or at least minimized by preparation. Some of these situations follow.

HOW TO AVOID UNKEPT APPOINTMENTS

Discrepancies between the time the caller is told to come in and the time he is actually seen by the executive can cause a great deal of discontent. If after hurrying to arrive for a one o'clock appointment, the caller finds that the executive is not available and cannot see him until two-thirty, he will be annoyed and upset. Most people are very understanding about emergency situations that delay appointments, but when the executive makes a practice of always being late, it conveys an impression of disorganization and carelessness. The fact that the executive's waiting room is very busy does not make people feel confident about an executive's ability.

There is generally no need to have long waits if a little time and foresight are put into the setting up of appointment schedules.

EFFECTIVE SCREENING OF TELEPHONE CALLS AVOIDS PROBLEMS

Another area that can cause strain is when the executive receives a telephone call during a meeting. It is often very difficult for an executive to take calls during meetings and it is important for the secretary to be able to convince the caller to agree to having the executive return the call.

For example:

> Your employer, Martha Schwartz, is in a meeting with the president of the company and has left word with you that she is not to be disturbed. Richard Murphy, a very important client, calls and demands to be put in touch with Martha immediately. You have a problem because Richard knows that the meeting is in session and that Martha is in the office.

You say, "Mr. Murphy, I am going to get a message to Ms. Schwartz as soon as possible and she will get back to you as soon as she can. Let me have the number where you can be reached within the next half hour or so."

By handling this call in this manner, you have shown yourself to be aware of the needs of the caller. Most people want to be treated fairly and courteously, and if they are treated in this manner consistently, the results will be increased satisfaction with the company. The following checklist will assist you in treating people well, which will increase your telephone effectiveness.

CHECKLIST FOR MAXIMIZING YOUR TELEPHONE EFFECTIVENESS

1. Answer promptly (by second or third ring).
2. Identify the office and yourself.
3. Convey pleasant and sincere tone.
4. Handle transfers smoothly and skillfully.
5. Explain if you have to put caller on hold, and return as soon as possible with the information or an explanation (never leave a caller on hold more than a minute without checking back).
6. Be helpful if person called is unavailable.
7. Have message pad and pen handy.
8. Record complete, accurate messages.
9. Close calls courteously.
10. Let the caller terminate the call.

AVOIDING CONFLICTS

It is essential to the practice of good human relations to avoid conflicts. The best way to avoid conflicts is to avoid confrontations. Although many times we confront or face a problem in order to solve it, this is not the same as confrontation in the practice of human relations.

For example, we all know that there are times when a boss may say to you "When Miss Blanco calls, I do not want to talk to her." You, as secretary, certainly would not confront Miss Blanco with this information when she calls. Instead, you would probably say something like, "I'm sorry Miss Blanco, Mrs. Diego is not in her office. May I take a message." When Miss Blanco calls again, you would probably say, "No, Mrs. Diego has not returned, but I certainly will see that she gets your message."

This type of avoidance of confrontation avoids conflict. A secretary should be aware of this technique when dealing with people. If you know that two co-workers do not get along, you certainly would not assign them to the same job to work together. When talking to one of them and asking his opinion, you would not continually quote the other worker's opinion as this would probably annoy the person to whom you are speaking.

This is really just practicing good common sense, but that sometimes is easier said than done because there is tremendous strain involved in trying to keep everyone happy and working as a team in harmony.

WRAPPING UP

Human relations cannot be taught the same way that stenography, typing, and bookkeeping are taught. It is the total of daily relationships with other people. Be careful not to prejudge people. Put your own feelings aside and practice good human relations.

Remember, that all people deserve to be treated with respect. You adjust your method to individual temperament, not to job or social status. This is a mistake many secretaries make. Naturally, you cannot leave a very important client waiting while you spend a great deal of time explaining to some members of the maintenance staff how you want some wiring done for the new word processor you are ordering. This situation could be handled in this manner:

> You cannot allow yourself to get flustered—all these people are important to your firm—you need to keep them all willing and happy to do business with you. All you

really need to do is say something to the maintenance staff like, "I see my boss's next appointment has come in. I'll be right back as soon as I talk with him and see if he can wait a few minutes."

To the client, you can say something like, "Good morning, Mr. Trent. So nice to see you. Could you bear with us a few moments, I am expecting delivery of some new equipment and the electricians are here to find out what must be done."

Most people are very willing to cooperate as long as they have some idea what is happening and that they are not being left waiting because of inconsideration on the part of others.

11

Better Management of Social Relationships

Recreation is very important to all of us. We are all familiar with the old saying, "All work and no play makes Jack a dull boy." Well, that holds true for all of us. If, as a secretary, you are dull, you certainly will not be able to practice human relations successfully. You will not be able to do your job properly and support your boss efficiently.

It is easy to say that recreation is important, but managing your recreation and your social relationships sometimes is not that easy. You must plan for your recreation just as you plan for your work day and be realistic in your approach to recreation. Think about the type of recreation you like, and choose activities that you are realistically able to do and that are not "tension building" in themselves.

For example:

> Susan loves to ski, but it seems that she doesn't get to go skiing more than once or twice during the winter. This year she decided to join a ski club. The group goes on two ski weekends a month and meets after work one evening a week to make plans. The group meets at the homes of the various members. Susan also attends college two evenings a week taking courses to complete her Bachelor of Business Administration degree.

BALANCING WORK AND PLAY

Susan loves the ski trips and enjoys the people in the club. But she now finds that between her job, her school work, and the club, she is feeling very pressured. What happened? Susan took on too much. With this particular ski club the program is much too ambitious for someone with Susan's business and education responsibilities, so the addition of the ski club activities has added more "work" and stress instead of providing her with recreation and relaxation. Susan should have chosen a different type of activity or if she wanted one that was ski-related, she should have found a different type or cut down her involvement in this one.

Often when we take on a leisure-time activity, it becomes so complicated that it hardly seems worth the effort. For instance, in Susan's case, if she tries to cut down her involvement in the club to perhaps attending one ski weekend a month and one meeting a month, she may find that the other members get annoyed with her because they need the full *support* of all their members in order to keep their club going.

SOCIAL RELATIONSHIPS ARE ESSENTIAL

If the other members are annoyed, Susan is not going to have the enjoyable relationship with them that she wants, which is essential to her feeling of well-being in the ski club. Susan will have to find a way to "support" their activities or else find another activity. Perhaps she could do some typing or arranging for the club without having to attend every meeting.

Social relationships are essential for all of us. No matter what our hobbies or interests are, it is usually important for us to share them with others. The degree of sharing will differ with individuals. For instance, taking the example of the ski club, some members may want and need their weekly meeting in order to maintain not only the club's responsibilities but also their own social needs.

But, in Susan's case, as much as she may want it, she must be realistic and see that she must manage her time and social relationships in such a way as to be able to balance all her activities.

SOCIALIZING WITH THE BOSS

You and your boss spend a great deal of time together—probably more time than either of you spend with family and friends. The boss/secretary relationship is a very special one. You, as the secretary, are in the position to become your boss's confidant. You manage the affairs of the office, you represent your boss and your office in many situations, and you spend a great deal of time with your boss receiving instructions, discussing work, and so forth. It is very easy for both of you to cross the line from business to social. But, you must be very careful to do your best to keep the relationship professional—a business relationship, not a social one. This may become increasingly difficult due to the nature of your job, but actually, you are in control and must be continuously aware of keeping the relationship businesslike.

There are many boss/secretary combinations. The most common still is the boss being a man and the secretary a woman.

If your boss starts asking you to lunch or dinner to talk over business or work on a project, do not always be available. Have other prior commitments. They may be perfectly legitimate meetings but it is best to avoid the "opportunity" to become too familiar and friendly, because the relationship can move very quickly from that of boss/secretary to that of friend and the pressure of conducting business with a friend is too difficult.

If you are a man and your boss is a woman, the same type of situation can easily develop. Even if the secretary and the boss are both men or both women, the problem of dealing with a friend in a business environment still exists. A boss can issue instructions to a secretary, but may find it difficult to issue the same instructions to a friend. You, the secretary, can receive orders from a boss, but may find it difficult to do so from a friend. Therefore, it is better to set the pattern from the beginning as that of a business relationship. If you must on occasion deal with your boss on a social level such as at a party or reception, you will be able to handle it easily if you control the situation yourself.

SOCIALIZING WITH BOSS'S SPOUSE

This is one of the most difficult relationships that you can enter into and you are best advised not to ever put yourself in that position. You work for your boss and your loyalty is to your boss. If you start to socialize with the boss's spouse, even on the telephone, you are leaving yourself open for questions and discussion concerning your boss that can only land you in trouble.

For example:

> Your boss asked you to pick out a blouse for his wife for her birthday. Your boss's wife calls up on her birthday to speak to her husband. You, knowing it is her birthday, say, "Happy Birthday." This may lead your boss's wife to say "Thank you, but how did you know?" You then have to say that your boss told you. In fact, you have opened the door for her to say, "I bet you picked out the blouse he gave me. I wondered where he got the idea for this type of blouse."

All this may seem unimportant, but the feeling has been left that the boss discusses his wife with his secretary and this is not always good. In fact, it may lead your boss's wife to asking you questions about your boss that you would rather not answer.

SOCIALIZING WITH OTHER BUSINESS ASSOCIATES

This also can be a problem and if you can avoid it, you should do so. If a situation arises in which you accept an invitation from an associate of your boss, you should make your boss aware of this because if you do not and it comes to light later, it may appear that you are hiding the relationship and your boss may become annoyed or read more into the situation than there really is. Your boss may feel that you are passing on confidential information that belongs only in your office.

SOCIALIZING WITH FRIENDS

Having friends is, of course, very important. Do not ever become so busy with your job that you give up your friends. Make certain that you allow time to spend with friends. But do not get in the habit of discussing business with your friends. If they do not know the people in your office, they will be thoroughly bored listening to a run down of your day or the gossip in your office, and you will probably lose them as friends.

If, on the other hand, you have friends who work with you or know the people in your office, another danger exists. They will probably be very interested in hearing office gossip. *DO NOT GOSSIP!* You can only suffer from it. Even if you swear a friend to secrecy, the information may leak out. In fact, get in the habit of not talking about business and you won't get into trouble. You will find that sometimes the most innocent remarks can cause problems.

For example:

> You have a date with a friend for lunch. You arrive late because your boss has had you change a letter at the last moment because he was not able to make up his mind about a bid on a contract.
>
> You excused your lateness to your friend by telling her the story—not realizing that you have put your friend in possession of a piece of information that she could give to her boss so that he could underbid your boss.

You should *not* have discussed business at all, but just indicated that you got stuck with something at the last moment.

Instead, your friend is faced with a problem. Should she tell her boss? Her loyalty is both to her boss and to her friend. If she doesn't tell her boss, it will be useless for him to make a bid. If she does and the bid is changed, her boss will get the business, but she will probably lose a friend and moreover, her boss may think that even though this worked out advantageously this time, next time he may be the one who suffers. Business confidences should not be discussed over lunch with friends.

SOCIALIZING WITH RELATIVES

To be a good secretary, you must be a happy, well-balanced person. When there are not enough hours in the day to do all we want to do, we often take the time away from the people who will understand, often the family. But a whole new set of pressures builds up because we feel guilty for not living up to family commitments and carry these guilty feelings and pressures over to our job. Our families will sometimes exert pressure on us, *but* if we are feeling guilty because we know that we have not done the right thing, then it will cause us even more concern.

For example:

> Maryanne's mother and father like her to come to dinner on Thursday evenings. Maryanne also looks forward to visiting with them, but the last few Thursday evenings she has received various invitations that she has not been able to pass up. Now she is looking forward to this Thursday and her boss has asked her to work on a special job. When she called her mother and cancelled again, her mother got very angry and told her that she is upsetting her father who has not been well.

Maryanne felt so bad about this that she was sharp with the people with whom she was working. She resented working and transferred her guilt to these people. This was unfair because, had she lived up to her commitments with her family earlier, she would have been able to take the Thursday night to work. The fault was hers and she was allowing it to affect her relationship with the people in the office.

CHOOSING FRIENDS

Your choice of friends is very important. Friendships do not just happen; they have to be cultivated. While we have many friendships during our lifetime, we sometimes outgrow earlier relationships and we must always be aware of this. We can and should keep old friends, but we must look carefully at the various relationships we make and see them in perspective.

Friends we had at school can and will continue to be good friends if we learn to see the friendship in the right perspective. We both may have changed and no longer share the same interests. With working all day, perhaps attending evening courses, and taking care of our various family commitments, we do not have much spare time. The time we have we enjoy spending with people who like to do the things we like to do. To have a friend visit museums with us just to please us is not beneficial to either of us. The friendship will suffer. We must both enjoy what we are doing. That is not to say we do not occasionally do things to please others, but we are discussing here a continuing situation. For example:

> Jeanne works as a secretary in an art gallery. She loves the art world and looked for quite a while for the right position in this field. Prior to this, she had worked for ten years in a bank. During that time, she had become very friendly with Maureen. The two women had worked closely together, ate lunch together every day, and occasionally went out socially on weekends. Now that Jeanne, through her job, has entree into art-associated functions and as she misses Maureen's company, she invites her regularly to go with her. The outings have not been a success. Jeanne is becoming more and more deeply involved in the world of art. Maureen really only goes to please her friend. She is studying to become a financial analyst and her interest is in this area. The friendship between the two women is in jeopardy.

Actually both women should examine the situation and realize that circumstances have changed. They can still be good friends, but not on such a constant day-to-day basis as when they worked together. Both must look for other friends that share their interests.

CHOOSING SOCIAL ACTIVITIES

Choosing social activities is just as important as choosing friends. You must enjoy your social activities and be in control of your own situation. Otherwise, you may find yourself not enjoying the kinds of things in which you are engaged. We have so many associations—family, friends, acquaintances, business associates—all of whom call on us for various social engagements. We have a limited amount of free time in which to engage in social activities, and we must make sure that we use it properly. Generally speaking, social activities should be pleasurable and something that we really want to do. Often, though, we are obligated as a result of our many associations to participate in social events that we would not have chosen for ourselves. This is all right as long as we are careful to always keep things in perspective and balance our events carefully so that we do not find ourselves spending every weekend involved in social activities in which we have no interest. The following guidelines for planning your free time should be helpful.

GUIDELINES FOR PLANNING YOUR FREE TIME

1. Do something *you* enjoy.
2. Decide whether to go alone or with friends.
3. Choose something where you can make new friends.
4. Decide how much time you can spend.
5. Decide how much money you can afford to spend.
6. Choose an activity that will be relaxing.
7. Decide whether the effort involved is worthwhile.
8. Make plans in advance.
9. Talk it over with friends.
10. Make a checklist of things to do beforehand.

MANAGING VACATION TIME

Vacations are very important for anyone and particularly for a person who spends seven or eight hours every day, five days a week working. Your vacation time is precious and should be carefully planned; otherwise, you may find that it disappears without your getting the rest and relaxation you need. You may decide to spend your vacation at home just relaxing and catching up on things you need to do. But, even if you stay at home, you must plan your activities to some degree, otherwise the time will just disappear and you will return to work feeling frustrated that you did not do what you had intended to do. Make a schedule for yourself that you can reasonably adhere to and you will find that you feel more relaxed.

> Beth took one week of her vacation to paint her kitchen. She also wanted to spend some time just relaxing, catching up on her reading. She decided to read and relax before she painted and it was Thursday before she got around to thinking about painting. By now she was pretty nervous because she had postponed thinking about the fact that she had to paint and the week was half over. So what was happening? Beth not only had not painted, but she also had not relaxed because she was worrying. Beth should have made herself a plan like the one in figure 11-1.

Of course, if you are going to travel on your vacation, it is obvious to you that you must plan ahead so that you can avoid any last minute delay and so that you will enjoy all of your vacation.

TRAVELING

Your vacation should be a source of fun and relaxation. However, it can be a potentially stressful situation too if you fail to do careful advance planning. Make a list of everything that you possibly can think of that you can do ahead. This will lessen that last minute mad rush that can result in your staying up all night and beginning your vacation tired. The following checklists will give you some ideas of what *your* checklists should include.

First, to help you decide where you want to go:

1. read travel literature
2. see a travel agent
3. decide what you can afford to spend
4. decide on length of stay
5. decide whether you will be traveling alone or with someone

BETTER MANAGEMENT OF SOCIAL RELATIONSHIPS 175

Before the trip, these tips will help you to make your own checklist of must-do tasks.

1. Update your passport.
2. Arrange for transportation and hotels.
3. Do research about the climate, type of clothing, etc.
4. Take care of pre-vacation shopping.
5. Make sure clothes are cleaned and ready.
6. Make a list of everything to be packed for the trip.
7. Begin packing a week in advance.

Figure 11-1

8. Obtain traveler's checks and cash, or convert your money into foreign currency.
9. Obtain travel guides, books, and maps well in advance.
10. Read and study guides and books as much as possible before you go.

WEEKEND, HOLIDAY, AND EVENING SOCIALIZING

Every bit of free time you have is very important to you and you should plan ahead for all of your time off. Do not wait until the weekend to decide what to do if you are the kind of person who does not like to be alone and always likes to have something to do. If you wait for the weekend or holiday or evening to come before you decide, you may find that you waste time making calls and trying to decide.

Of course, you do not have to have every moment planned. You may prefer not having any arrangements made. But *you* have to decide what kind of person you are. If you do not want to spend your free time alone or looking for something to do, you must plan ahead.

MARRIED OR SINGLE

Whether you are married or single, managing your social relationships is very important. The single person is often more aware of this than the married person because a married person may think, "I am not alone—there are two of us and we have plenty to do at home, so we don't need to worry about vacation, travel, or going out." But that is not the case. You must have leisure time, socialize with others, and do things other than work.

KEY FACTORS IN PLANNING YOUR LEISURE ACTIVITIES

Use your leisure time to the best advantage. Not only can leisure activities provide many enriching experiences, but they can serve to make you a well-rounded person. Even more important, such activities serve to make you a happier, more productive employee. Having spent an enjoyable evening or weekend can be just the change needed from the often humdrum office routine. You will return to the office with a fresh outlook, as if you had been away on vacation.

Leisure activities can also provide enrichment through participation in courses, clubs, or recreational activities that involve you in learning something new. As a result, you will be a more interesting conversationalist, you will be more up to date about current events, and you will make new friends.

Developing your personality is a very real benefit of social interaction. An attractive personality will certainly be an asset in the business office, where you are meeting new people and interacting daily. You will not only gain polish and sophistication through varied leisure activities, you will gain valuable experience in dealing with the many different types of personalities you encounter in the business world.

WRAPPING UP

A good balance between work and play has always been a good prescription for happiness. If you are happy in your social life, you will probably be better able to deal with the problems of your work-a-day world. The person who, along with the requisite job knowledge and skill, is able to deal effectively with people on both a social and business level has a big "plus" for getting ahead in a chosen career.

12

Successful Participation in Office Social Life

No one can be "all business" all the time. Every office has its social life—some more than others. Many large firms have recreation facilities for their employees such as libraries, TV rooms, exercise rooms, card rooms, game rooms, and so forth. Often there are company bowling and softball teams. We are all familiar with office holiday parties and, if you are a member of a firm that does not make a concerted effort to accommodate the office social life, there is still the coffee break and lunch break and occasional dinners or theater visits with friends you have made among co-workers.

In as much as a person spends so much of the day at the job, the job chosen must be a pleasant one. A person must feel comfortable and enjoy some social time in order to put forth the best effort at work.

But one must achieve the proper balance in handling office social life. There are times you can be social and times you must avoid being too friendly; you must be able to distinguish between them.

For example:

> Susan James is secretary to the manager of customer relations, Joe Phillips. Joe calls her Susan and tells her to

call him by his first name. One day the President of the firm is in Joe's office with an important customer who has filed a complaint. Joe calls Susan in to find correspondence for him. Susan gets it immediately and he says, "Thanks, Susan. That's great. You're so efficient." Susan is so pleased and responds, "Oh, thank you, Joe."

Later after the President and the customer have left, Joe calls Susan in and reprimands her for calling him Joe in front of the President and customer.

Susan is very upset. She feels that Joe calls her "Susan" and after all he did tell her to call him, "Joe." She is really right, but he is the boss and she should realize that in front of others he may not want to be addressed so informally. In fact, it is always a good idea to keep things on a more formal basis in front of others.

There are many times in the office situation where it is difficult to know what the right behavior is—but if you always remember that it is a business office, not a home, you may find it a help.

You may be very friendly with a group of secretaries in the office and you always eat lunch together and often see each other on weekends or after work. For example:

You are the secretary to the personnel manager and as such, are privy to a lot of information about other people in the office. Your close friend, another secretary in the firm, has been turned down for the raise she had requested. You tell her this in strictest confidence because she asks you and she is your friend.

She is so upset that she runs into her boss's office and wants to know why she has been turned down. Of course, her boss knows where she got the information, because it is well known that you are friends.

This whole situation is very upsetting and could have been avoided if both you and your friend had followed the rule that even though you are friends, you must remember to behave in a businesslike manner when in the office and keep business matters separate from your social activities.

SOCIAL RELATIONSHIPS WITH CUSTOMERS AND CLIENTS

Another area that is very sensitive is social relationships with customers and clients. In your role as secretary, you meet all kinds of people who come into the office to see your employer. Often you may be invited to dinner or some other social event. It is wise to be very careful about encouraging social relationships with these people. Naturally you may be very attracted to someone and want to accept an invitation. You really should let your employer know that you are going to see the customer or client outside the office so that your employer does not feel that you may be acting against company interests. For example:

> Sam Johnstone, a salesman for a metal parts company has been trying to get your firm's business for a long time. He comes to your office several times a month to see your boss. He usually spends a few minutes chatting with you and you find you have mutual interests. Sam invites you to dinner and you accept. Another salesman happens to see you and mentions to your boss that he guesses there is no chance of his getting the contract with Sam "wining and dining the secretary."
>
> Your boss gets a phone call from his superior questioning whether or not this is so. Your boss is very annoyed with you for putting him in this position.

This could all have been avoided if you had told your boss about the invitation in the first place.

THE OFFICE PARTY

Many companies frown on office parties because of the problems with improper behavior that may occur. On the other hand, an office party, if planned properly, can be very beneficial to the morale of the staff and certainly there are many functions that you as a secretary may be responsible for planning such as business luncheons, retirement dinners, and awards ceremonies.

Lists are an indispensible aid in planning any kind of party whether it is an informal office party, a business luncheon, or a formal retirement dinner for one of your boss's colleagues. Where do you begin?

Depending on the kind of party being given, preliminary discussions with those in charge, for example your boss, or an entertainment committee will determine the ground rules.

BASIC PLANNING CONSIDERATIONS
[PRELIMINARY CHECKLIST]

size
space
time
day
menu
cost
drinks
entertainment
decorations
speaker
special seating
special awards

Your preliminary checklist will look like the one above. After these basic decisions have been made, and you have gone over everything with your boss or the group planning the party, several more checklists will be needed. You may begin with:

Advance Planning (2 to 3 weeks before)

One week before

Day before

Day of the Party

The lists will be similar and will actually be revisions of the first list. Each new list will break down into more detail those items that call for it. For instance:

the menu

seating and table arrangement

decorating

entertainment

speaker and awards

special lighting and audiovisual equipment

Lists will help you to organize and delegate tasks so that everything does not fall on you. Last minute decisions will be minimized because you have done careful advance planning. Put everything down on lists, but revise your lists carefully and recheck everything to be certain everything has been included. Go over each list with the person in charge of that aspect of the party.

CHECKLIST FOR ADVANCE PLANNING

1. Finalize guest list.
2. Decide when and what type of invitations to send.
3. Finalize menu.
4. Decide on decorations.
5. Decide on entertainment.
6. Plan the order of the program.
7. Set up ceremony involving speaker and/or guests
8. Order awards well in advance (in case of special engraving, etc.)
9. Arrange for audio-visual and lighting.
10. Decide on honorarium for speaker.

PARTICIPATING IN GROUP ACTIVITIES ... COMPANY CLUBS, TEAMS, CLASSES

Think through any ideas for new social activities before starting anything. Explore all the pros and cons first. Would it be good for the employees? Would it interfere with the company? How would it benefit the company? For example:

> Shari and a few of her co-workers decided that they would like to utilize part of their lunch hour to get some much needed exercise. It really started as a spur-of-the-moment idea with five of the secretaries who were sitting around talking after lunch one day. They just started doing a few easy exercises that did not even involve changing clothes.

However, after only two days, the supervisor heard about it and immediately put a stop to it. He called the group together and told them that someone could be injured and that the company would be liable for any injuries received on the job.

Shari and the others were really disappointed. It had all begun innocently enough without any thought of it harming anyone. In fact, they even felt that they would be better able to perform on the job after exercising. They would be wide awake and have more energy during the afternoon for doing their work. However, they hadn't thought it through nor had they cleared the way by going through the proper channels to get permission.

The idea was a good one and the response from co-workers was enthusiastic, both of which are important to the success of starting a new program. But the correct procedure is to get approval from your boss and authorization from the proper sources. Once these preliminaries are out of the way, then you can proceed along lines similar to those in the next checklist.

CHECKLIST FOR STARTING A NEW CLUB OR PROGRAM

1. Discuss the idea and think it through with others.
2. Get approval to proceed from your employer and those in authority.
3. Be willing to bear the brunt of the responsibility—paper work, setting up meetings, refreshments, etc.
4. Circulate a flyer or questionnaire to find out how many are interested. [figure 12-1]
5. Call meeting at a convenient time. [figure 12-2]
6. Elect officers.
7. Plan a program and schedule regular times to meet.

HANDLING COLLECTIONS FOR GIFTS

Handling money and taking up collections for gifts can be touchy, especially in a situation where people from many different backgrounds are involved. Use caution and try to be

September 15, 19__

TO: Everyone
FROM: Shari, Maria, and Pat
SUBJECT: Exercise Class

Jean Parsons in Word Processing conducts an exercise class at a community center on weekends. She has agreed to conduct one here if we want it.

Are you interested?

        Yes [ ]   No [ ]   Maybe [ ]

Time?

Lunch time	11:45-12:15	[ ]
Before work	8:15- 8:45	[ ]
After work	5:00- 5:30	[ ]
Another time	[ ]	[ ]

Please give answer by Tuesday to Shari so that we can get plans under way.

Figure 12-1 Questionnaire for Exercise

SUCCESSFUL PARTICIPATION IN OFFICE SOCIAL LIFE

September 20, 19__

TO: Everyone
FROM: Shari, Maria, and Pat
RE: <u>Exercise Class</u>

The response to our flyer was terrific. Twenty people said they were interested.

Please attend a meeting in the west conference room at 12:15 Tuesday to finalize plans, form a committee, and elect officers.

Mr. Pauling has given us approval to go ahead on this.

Figure 12-2 Meeting Notice

September 21, 19__

TO: Everyone

FROM: Tanya Oliva (for the Committee)

RE: <u>Special Occasion Fund</u>

It's time again to replenish our gift fund. This time we are requesting a $5 donation. Please see me with your contribution.

Since last time we bought gifts for:

  Elena Guttierez—wedding

  Dorothy Janus—baby boy

  Phillip Petrie—retirement

  John Wellington—operation- get well

Please keep me advised of special occasions. Thank you.

Figure 12-3 Notice for Special Occasion Fund

very fair. An easy way to do it would be to set up a "Special Occasion Fund." Remember, if you are the secretary to the head of the department you should delegate this to someone else, otherwise the other employees may feel pressured because they feel that the request is coming from your employer. In fact, if the department or group is large enough, a committee is a very good idea. Contributions to the "Special Occasion Fund" should be voluntary, with everyone given the opportunity to contribute to it. However, no one should be criticized for not contributing. Periodically a notice can be sent to everyone requesting a contribution. The employees can be instructed to give their contributions to a particular person but no one should be reminded if they do not give (see figure 12-3). One very easy way to be certain that everyone is included is to have a checklist of all the names so that each can be checked off as a notice is sent. Also when money is taken up periodically, the checklist can be used to check off the names of those who contributed. When a gift is sent, the card should not list individual names, just something general, such as "Accounting Department."

ACCEPTING GIFTS—DO'S AND DON'TS

There is a time and place for everything and there are times when it is all right for the secretary to accept a gift from the boss or from colleagues. Special occasions that call for gifts are holidays, weddings, and births. However, giving and receiving gifts should be played down as much as possible. It is certainly appropriate to show your appreciation, but do it discreetly with an expression of sincere thanks and a handwritten note. It is all right to accept gifts from your boss, but if one of your boss's clients tries to give you a gift for doing a favor, it is best to decline it by saying something like, "Oh, that's all right, Mr. Thomas, I was glad to do it, but I really can't accept anything for it. Thanks anyway." However, if the client gives the gift to your boss to pass on to you, it would be all right to accept it from your boss.

It is fine to accept gifts from your colleagues as long as they don't interfere with your work. The giving and receiving should be kept completely separate from the regular routine of the business day.

WRAPPING UP

Office social life is just as important to the office as office business life, but it is important to be aware of when it is acceptable to apply the rules of social behavior and when business behavior must be followed. The line between the two is very fine and sometimes hard to discern, so in order to be able to comfortably participate in the office social life and still maintain proper business behavior, you must be sensitive to what is expected of you.

13

Strategies for Dealing with Tough Office Situations

Often we have so much to communicate to someone that we are not sensitive to their needs and desires and so do not achieve our goal of getting our message across. Instead of communicating, our message falls on deaf ears.

For example:

> Marilyn, a corresponding secretary in the Word Processing Department, is getting married. Jennifer is very fond of Marilyn and is arranging a party for her. She has chosen the restaurant, and decided on the day and how much each person should contribute. All this has been a great deal of work and Jennifer is very surprised to find that people are grumbling about the cost of the party and are declining to go. She is upset and feels that this is a definite affront to Marilyn.
>
> What Jennifer fails to realize is that the problem began with her and although Marilyn is suffering from it, Jennifer could have avoided this by remembering that effective communication is not just taking over and getting your own way but in listening to what other people have to say.
>
> She could have written a memorandum and distributed it to the department telling them what she was planning and asking for input before she went ahead. This way communicating is not a one-way street.

GETTING ALONG WITH SUPERIORS

As communication is a two-way street, keeping the lines of communication open with your superior will be easy if you are open and honest and able to take criticism without taking offense. You have probably already found that the more relaxed and natural you are with your boss, the better your relationship will be.

The following checklist will help improve communication between you and your boss.

1. Find out your boss's preferences.
2. Listen to what is said.
3. Be cooperative.
4. Be flexible.
5. Be open.
6. Be honest.
7. Be direct.
8. Set aside your own personal desires and problems.
9. Be thorough.
10. See a job through to completion.

Your boss's success is important to you, because your boss's advancement means ultimate success for you.

Learn as much as you can about the business the firm conducts so that you can discuss it intelligently. Your understanding of the firm will make you more confident about assuming some of the responsibilities that your boss would like to delegate. This can free your boss to concentrate on other important business.

Leave your own personal problems at home. Discussing problems concerning your children with your boss will not accomplish anything. In fact, it could put you in a bad light, so the less said the better. On the other hand, if your boss wants to talk to you about personal problems, you may have to listen, but without commenting. Just lending an ear often helps.

It doesn't hurt to compliment your boss on an accomplishment. Congratulations are always in order. However, you should not make yourself conspicuous by going out of your way, but if the right moment comes along, then it is appropriate to say something such as, "Congratulations, Mr. Decker, on your promotion."

COOPERATE WITH CO-WORKERS

It is important to get along with everyone, especially your fellow workers. Cooperation is a key element in running an efficient office. A good relationship with co-workers may mean that you are willing to help each other out and work together when the need arises. Often special projects demand teamwork on the part of everyone.

Be a good listener. Take time to exchange pleasantries. Appear to be interested even if your mind is on other things. If you are always in a hurry or appear disinterested, your co-workers will soon get the message and quit making any effort to relate to you. Your position as secretary/administrative assistant makes it imperative for you to get along with all employees. Often you have to carry your boss's instructions to them and have the responsibility of seeing that the work is done. If your relations with co-workers are not the best, they will not be willing to help you get *your* job done.

For example:

> Gina is a young secretary just out of college and working for John Fairfax, the financial director of the firm. He needs to have certain figures from the accountants by Friday to complete various statements. He commissions Gina to see to it that these figures reach him on time saying to her that Bill Thomas really needs a push because he is so slow.
>
> She goes to the accountants and tells them that she needs the figures by Friday and that Mr. Fairfax says for Bill to particularly hurry up because he is so slow.

What has happened here? Gina has alienated the accountants. How?

> 1. She gave them the impression that it was she who was issuing the instructions, not Mr. Fairfax. That only irri-

tated them even though they, in fact, knew that it was Mr. Fairfax's work. This gave them the feeling that she was "power-hungry."

2. She told them that Mr. Fairfax said one among their ranks, Bill Thomas, is slow. If he talks about Bill, he probably talks about all of them. Why should he tell her derogatory things about them instead of speaking to them directly? Why should she know he feels this way and why has he chosen to allow them to find out this way? If he thinks their work is not up to par, they have not had any inkling about it before.

Gina has accomplished several things by not carefully choosing her words and evaluating her role as secretary/assistant before speaking to the accountants.

1. They are annoyed now and also feel insecure in their position.
2. They feel resentment toward Mr. Fairfax because they have found out he is not satisfied with their work.
3. They do not like him speaking to others about their faults rather than directly to them.
4. They resent a secretary issuing orders to them.
5. Gina will probably *not* be able to get the figures to her boss on time.

BE COURTEOUS WITH BUSINESS ASSOCIATES

Getting along with your employer's business associates is extremely important. You cannot afford to play favorites with anyone, even though you may know one person better and be aware that their relationship to your firm is very profitable. Treat everyone who calls or comes into the office with equal courtesy and friendliness.

Everyone should receive equal treatment whether the individual is from within the firm or is an outsider. You can promote your boss, and yourself as well, by being friendly and helpful to associates within the firm.

For example:

> Janet was recommended for a promotion by another executive within the firm who observed her performance on two particular occasions. On one occasion she volunteered to stay late to place a call for one of her boss's associates and on another occasion she researched something and typed it up for her boss and an associate. When an opening came for a district coordinator for the firm, Janet was one of the people considered.

In addition to her boss's endorsement, the associate also recommended her highly. This dual recommendation from two management people ensured Janet's appointment.

You may have to force yourself to be friendly at times, especially when you are not feeling up to par. Such an occasion might be when a client comes in that you know your boss would rather not see. This may really tax your ability not to show your true feelings. You are not being dishonest; you are just displaying tact and diplomacy when it is most needed. The following checklist will help you develop skill in handling difficult situations.

CHECKLIST FOR DEALING WITH DIFFICULT SITUATIONS

1. Remain calm.
2. Be pleasant.
3. Treat everyone fairly, courteously, and with respect.
4. Think before you act.
5. Examine all sides of an issue.
6. Deal with the situations in a straightforward and tactful manner.

KEEPING UP TO DATE WITH COLLEAGUES

Most business and professional people keep up to date on current happenings in the business world and particularly within their own field of interest by membership in professional organizations, attendance at conferences and seminars, reading of business news in both newspapers and professional journals, and participation in continuing education programs. Interaction with their colleagues is of prime concern to their pursuit of professionalism.

You as a secretary/assistant have professional organizations to which you can belong. Memberships in organizations such as these enable you to meet and talk with people who have positions similar to yours and who have an active interest in furthering business and professional relationships.

The same human relations skills apply with colleagues as with co-workers. Your colleagues are those who occupy a similar position and/or carry the same rank as you do. Friendliness, tact, discretion, and diplomacy are the key elements in promoting good communications with them. Cooperation between colleagues is essential in maintaining open lines of communication.

CHECKLIST FOR MAINTAINING OPEN LINES OF COMMUNICATION

1. Maintain friendly relations.
2. Be open, honest, and direct.
3. Use tact and discretion.
4. Be flexible (willing to compromise).
5. Cooperate.

For example:

Mary Beth, secretary to the head of Pediatrics at General Hospital, is a member of a professional medical secretaries' association. Her boss is interested in conducting an "Outreach" program in the community to alert parents about the dangers of a certain contagious disease that may be approaching the locality within the next eight to ten weeks if proper preventive measures are not taken. Those most susceptible to this disease are children between the ages of 3 and 7. Mary Beth contacted her friend, a member of the local chapter of an educational organization, for aid in how to go about contacting the parents who had children in this age group and how to start such a program.

The assistance Mary Beth received from her friend enabled her to proceed in a very positive fashion in assisting her boss to achieve his goal. Not only did she help her boss and the community, but she also was able to demonstrate, in a very professional manner, her value as an administrative assistant. One of the organizations in which you as a secretary may have an interest is:

PSI (Professional Secretaries International)
300 East Armour Boulevard
Kansas City, MO 64111-7010

Some other organizations that may be of interest are:

American Association of Medical Assistants
National Association of Bank Women, Inc.
National Association of Education Secretaries
National Association of Legal Secretaries
The Business and Professional Women's Club

KEEP YOUR RELATIONSHIPS BUSINESSLIKE

Verbal communication between men and women in a work situation requires similar human relations skills. Each individual should be treated with respect. Courteousness, friendliness, and fairness are the hallmarks of maintaining good relations.

Caution and discretion will help to keep relationships businesslike. This is true for both men and women. Exercise caution in your conversation. Kidding can sometimes be taken the wrong way. It may be taken as flirting rather than friendliness, so watch what you say and how you say it.

Your dress is another key communicator. In the business office your clothes should reflect the atmosphere, surroundings, and type of business. Generally, conservative dress is best. Save the bright colors, and fancy or tight fitting outfits for your leisure time away from the office. Clothes that are not proper for the business setting can be distracting and may invite unwanted comments and looks.

Of course, even though you are careful about your speech and dress, maintaining a businesslike relationship in some instances may require extra effort on your part, especially when an individual is persistent in going beyond the point of a friendly relationship. An example would be:

> Susan, an attractive young secretary, is having a problem because her boss has displayed a very definite personal interest in her. He has asked her to have lunch with him several times and has insinuated that if she does not consent, her job might be in jeopardy.

Susan likes her job very much, but does not want this personal involvement with her boss. What should she do? Can the use of tact and diplomacy quickly put a halt to this situation? This is really a very difficult situation and has to be handled carefully. It is possible that Susan inadvertently gave her boss some idea that she was receptive to his personal interest in her. Before taking such drastic steps as reporting him to his superior or to the personnel department, it might make better sense to try a simpler approach. Susan could indicate that she has a fiance who would not approve of her having lunch with any other male companion. If the boss indicated that this was nonsense and that it is part of her job, Susan could indicate quite firmly that she liked her job and liked working for him, but if it meant that she had to go out socially with him to keep the job, she would have to resign. If the boss appears willing to accept the resignation or fire Susan, then it may be to her advantage to discuss this with the personnel manager or his superior. Some firms have counselors to help employees with problems such as these.

Situations like this are extremely difficult and the best solution is probably not a solution at all but "prevention." In the above case, the boss is a man and the secretary a woman. But even when the reverse is true, the same rules apply. Be very careful not to do anything that encourages your boss to feel you are in any way receptive to social involvement. This is the best course to follow because often if the situation reaches the point where you have to discuss it with your boss or take it to a superior, you may find that you will be more comfortable finding another job.

The whole issue of sexual harrassment has become so widely publicized today that it is very important that you stop and think through any situation before you act or in fact overreact. Make sure you are not reading into a situation something that is not so but also make sure you recognize the situation when it does exist. The following checklist is helpful:

CHECKLIST FOR MAINTAINING BUSINESSLIKE RELATIONSHIPS

1. Be courteous.
2. Treat each person with respect.
3. Exercise caution and discretion to avoid awkward situations or unwanted attention.
4. Dress conservatively.
5. Avoid social involvement with opposite sex unless it is a part of the business function.

DEALING WITH OTHER MEMBERS OF THE ORGANIZATION

Cooperation is essential to improving relationships, especially in business. Today with more and more emphasis being placed on improved production and reduction of costs, the secretary's role is becoming more important—representing the boss. You may have to coordinate and bring together the various people involved in a project so that everyone works together harmoniously to accomplish their tasks.

Essentially you are acting as liaison between your boss and others in the general production process whether they be other secretaries, word processors, mail clerks, records managers, or reprographics experts. Working with such a range of skilled and unskilled employees both directly and indirectly places an added burden on you to practice your human relations skills with a great deal of care and consideration for the individual, but always keep in mind the goals of your boss and firm.

For example:

> Lila is the secretary to Margaret Patterson, the editor of the company newsletter. Ms. Patterson is scheduled to be admitted into the hospital for surgery the middle of next month. The usual date for reviewing material for the

DEALING WITH TOUGH OFFICE SITUATIONS

newsletter is the second Wednesday of each month. Ms. Patterson wants to move the date up to the first Wednesday of the month. She tells you to take care of it and see that everyone involved is notified and that all material will be in.

Lila has a big human relations job on her hands because she is going to have to ask all those people involved to work double time to move up their deadlines. She must be very tactful and "get the people on her side." She cannot just issue the order but must first explain that it is coming from her boss and that she (Lila) needs their help so that she can get all the material to her boss on time.

It would, of course be best to tell them the reason why Ms. Patterson wants the information early. However, this may be confidential and Lila may have to generalize about the reason.

SPECIAL HINTS IF YOUR BOSS IS A WOMAN

Whether you are a woman working for a woman or a man working for a woman, you can benefit from the checklist below. *Remember,* women are generally more attuned to detail than men and often tend to involve themselves in the details of your work, rather than just telling you to do a job and leaving you free to do it. This can be annoying but it can also be beneficial. If you work for a person who is like this, you will find ways to exercise the practice of your human relations skills so that the job can get done with the least amount of conflict.

> Arthur is the secretary to the manager of the Accounting Department, Donna DiLeo. One of his duties is to keep the Employee's Accounting Manual updated with current rules and regulations, office policy changes, notification of formatting changes for statements, roster lists for receipt of statements, and various other information that would be of use to people preparing the various financial statements issued by the company.
>
> This is really rather routine because the memoranda affecting this come to Arthur after being okayed by Ms. DiLeo, and he just has to incorporate the information into the existing Manual. Ms. DiLeo, however, is very con-

cerned about this being done properly and keeps asking to see drafts of the material—much to Arthur's annoyance.

Actually, Arthur should recognize the fact that she is like this and understand that it really has nothing to do with his ability. Perhaps he should say something like, "Ms. DiLeo, I am going to input all these changes on my word processor and will return everything to you for your okay before it is released. Please feel free to change anything so that it is exactly the way you want, as it is no trouble for me to correct on the word processor." This way he is doing his job and letting her know that she can correct anything she wants without anyone getting upset.

CHECKLIST FOR GETTING ALONG WITH A DIFFICULT BOSS

1. Be sensitive to your boss's preferences.
2. Be flexible—able to adjust to different situations.
3. Do what your boss wants—no argument please.
4. Don't take things too seriously—seemingly unreasonable requests should not undermine your own faith in yourself.
5. Keep your boss up to date on everything—by notes, reminders on the calendar, memoranda, and copies of documents.
6. Maintain your own complete files of copies of everything just in case.
7. Don't allow yourself to become flustered.
8. Don't blame others—instead, look for alternative solutions.
9. Remind yourself to remain cool and calm.

STRATEGIES FOR DEALING WITH MATURE WORKERS

One of the biggest problem areas to the secretary is supervising older and more experienced people. This can be done easily, however, if you remember your role. You are acting for your boss, not giving orders for yourself. You are asking people to help you do your job, which is to carry out your boss's orders.

DEALING WITH TOUGH OFFICE SITUATIONS

Dorothy was responsible for having a 94-page report typed by the four typists in the department, all of whom were mature women. They were being asked to drop all their other work and get this report out in one day. Dorothy's boss, the Vice President of Administrative Services, had given her this assignment. Each typist was assigned to unit managers and had the responsibility of typing the work for the unit.

Dorothy, in her zeal to accomplish her task, went directly to each of the four women and told them to drop everything and do this work immediately. Naturally, everyone got excited and a crisis resulted. The women went to their managers who, in turn, went to Dorothy's boss and complained.

Dorothy should have planned her strategy carefully by first deciding on the format and distribution of work; then approaching the unit managers and enlisting their support, explaining the situation and showing them the plan and how she would assist the typists to get the job accomplished in the minimum amount of time. After getting their approval, she could have approached these women and told them of her dilemma. The chances are everyone would have been *willing* to assist and not felt forced into it. Everyone would have felt good about helping. Dorothy would have gotten her job done and her employer would have had the report he needed. The crisis that developed in the original handling of the situation would not have occurred, and the conflict that evolved would have been avoided.

DEALING EFFECTIVELY WITH CRISES

However, no matter how hard you try to avoid crisis situations, they do occur—often the situation occurs without your having a chance to prevent it. The following checklist is an aid in preventing a crisis and in handling it once it occurs.

Take a deep breath and think about what you must do. *Do not* just jump in and start "doing." Plan your strategy first.

CHECKLIST FOR PREVENTING A CRISIS

1. Think about what it is you want to accomplish.

2. List everything that has to be done from beginning to end.
3. Find out who will be working on the project.
4. Clear the way with each person who will be assisting by going through the proper channels to obtain permission and/or release them from other responsibilities.
5. Draw up your own detailed specifications (including format, time-frame, punctuation, grammar, capitalization, proofreading).
6. Establish priorities and deadlines.
7. Call the project team together and explain what the project involves and why they are being asked to help.
8. Make them aware that they are making a big contribution to the growth of the department and the company.
9. Divide the work among the members of the group, ask if there are any questions, and let them know that they can come to you with their questions.
10. Make yourself available for questions.

CREATING A GOOD WORKING ATMOSPHERE

You, as the secretary, have a responsibility to improve some of the business relationships by creating the best working atmosphere possible. This is a challenge because often it is the boss who sets the tone of the office. This is fine if the tone that is set is a good one, but often it is not because the boss may be overworked or too pressured to realize that the working atmosphere is not the best. It is then up to you to counteract this, because your job is as support to your boss and this is naturally a part of it. If the atmosphere is not conducive to getting the work done, your boss will suffer. Some things to remember are:

CHECKLIST FOR CREATING A GOOD WORKING ATMOSPHERE

1. Set a happy tone by being friendly and easy going.
2. Demonstrate a spirit of cooperation with colleagues.
3. Make the office as cheerful and attractive as possible.

DEALING WITH TOUGH OFFICE SITUATIONS

4. Organize activities so that things run smoothly.
5. Maintain a positive attitude.

ASSERTING YOURSELF

Handling difficult human relations situations that arise daily where people work in close proximity does not mean that you must think in terms of taking aggressive action. It may not even call for immediate confrontation of the situation. Just being aware of what is taking place and being able to recognize that there is a problem is *Step One*. From there, *Step Two* is looking at the situation as objectively as possible—examining all the possible alternatives—and then *Step Three* is deciding whether or not action is called for. If the answer is yes, *Step Four* involves deciding how to handle the situation in the best possible way.

Today, we hear a lot about women asserting themselves, which in simple everyday language is dealing effectively with a problem situation, usually involving communication and human relations skills. Success in this area is measured in terms of how well the problem is resolved. It may not involve any complex set of rules to work through. It usually means exercising good judgment, using discretion, being diplomatic in working out the problem, and finally standing firm on what you decide to do. The following checklist will help you to deal with problems more assertively.

CHECKLIST FOR DEALING ASSERTIVELY WITH PROBLEM SITUATIONS

1. State the problem.
2. Gather all of the facts.
3. Explore all of the possible options.
4. Talk over the options with someone.
5. Rehearse what you plan to say with another person or in front of a mirror.
6. Organize your plan into its final form.
7. Put your plan into effect.

Most of us are assertive in some situations, but not in others. In fact, you may even back off altogether with certain people or in certain situations.

TEST YOURSELF—CAN YOU ANSWER "YES" TO THE FOLLOWING QUESTIONS?

1. Can you say no without feeling guilty because you may be hurting someone else's feelings?
2. Can you handle conflicts or disagreements without getting upset to the point that it affects your work?
3. Do you know the difference between being assertive and being aggressive?
4. Do you say what you really mean or what the other person wants to hear?
5. Can you take criticism? How do you deal with it?
6. Are you direct and honest with your boss and co-workers?

DEALING EFFECTIVELY WITH DELICATE SITUATIONS

Try your hand at dealing with the following situations:

SITUATION I

You have two bosses and both have asked you to complete important assignments almost simultaneously. Do you tell them both that you cannot possibly do both jobs at once or do you play one against the other?

SITUATION II

You and another secretary have been assigned by your boss to work together on coordinating an important project, but as it turns out, you seem to be doing all the work. The other secretary has either been absent, delayed, or otherwise tied up with other things. How do you deal with the situation, especially when you know that you cannot possibly handle the project alone?

SITUATION III

You know how to streamline the word processing department so that the quantity and quality of the work will improve, but the office manager, your boss, who designed the system, takes any suggestions for change as personal criticism.

HOW TO GAIN ACCEPTANCE WITHOUT CREATING RESENTMENT

There are many ways that these situations could be handled effectively. Knowing the personalities of the people you deal with would have a direct bearing on how you solve them.

Some suggested ways to deal with these delicate human relations problems follow.

In the first instance where you are working for two bosses, you must make each boss aware of the work you have and indicate that you will get both jobs done but you cannot do both at once. Suggest that perhaps you might be given the authority to ask another secretary to assist you or that one of the jobs be delayed a short while until the other is done.

In Situation II, you should discuss this problem with the other secretary and have her understand that this is an assignment that you are both working on. As she has so many other things to do, perhaps both of you should talk to your boss about seeing that she is freed of her other assignments. Before you go to your boss though, perhaps both of you can look at the other work, analyze the problem, see how long the joint project will take and then present the facts to your boss. The other secretary may suddenly realize the importance of the project and discover that she is able to do her part. You will have gotten your message across without actually going to your boss, and you boss's wishes will have been carried out.

In Situation III where you want to streamline the word processing department you need to exercise diplomacy. Show your boss how well the system she designed is working, then indicate that if you implemented this "one other thing," it will be even better.

Take one thing at a time. Do not do an overall revamping of the system. Suggest one adjustment, always in a positive manner. This will make your system even better. Of course, make sure the change you are suggesting really is appropriate and that it is presented constructively. The chances are it will be accepted. Remember to present it as an additional improvement to the system not a change *from* the original system. You are then supporting your boss's ideas, not tearing them down. Statements such as "The system is working beautifully; we can get 20 memos out an hour and I am sure we could increase it to 30 if we staggered the coffee break time. What do you think? Is it worth a try?"

This way your boss is really being given the chance to decide and it will not be thought of as a criticism but a suggestion.

WRAPPING UP

In the final analysis, getting along with the people with whom you work should be taken seriously. It should be approached with a lot of thought and concern both for yourself and for others. The essential element is to try to improve relationships and show a willingness to learn—sometimes from your own mistakes. Above all, be aware of what is going on around you and concentrate on maintaining good relationships.

14

Creating a More Attractive You

Your impact on people is a total package—you must try to be sympathetic, understanding, sensitive to their wishes, caring, diplomatic, and willing to take action to help. You may possess all of these qualities but if your appearance is such that it does not attract people to you, you may never get a chance to practice your human relations skills.

We can all look good to others—a smile and a pleasant look are a big start. We may have to practice this. Haven't we all had a friend ask us "What's wrong?" and been startled because actually nothing was wrong. "What's wrong?" is that we probably have let our expressions fall into a frown or too serious a look. It is important to be aware of this because often a person will not approach you if you look too busy or harried or worried *or* too stern. If you always are careful to look approachable, people will be more willing to talk with you. In an office the "stern-looking" secretary will probably have difficulty dealing with people because they will be put off by her expression.

So, remember, be aware, practice your expression, notice how people respond to you and think about the reason why.

Of course, after the way you look comes the way you carry yourself. If you slump while walking or sit slumped over at your desk, you will not inspire confidence—you may look bored, uninterested, or even defeated.

The alert looking secretary sits up straight, walks purposefully, and always looks poised and capable.

Now that we are aware of facial expressions and body language, we can go on to clothing.

Inappropriate clothing can give a totally wrong impression. Remember, you cannot practice human relations skills until you have made a positive first impression. These three items of appearance all contribute to that very important "first impression":

1. facial expression
2. posture
3. clothing

If you do not "pass" on a first impression someone has of you, it is an uphill battle to change that impression. Why give yourself that problem? The key word is "awareness." How others see us *is* important on our job.

As unfair as it may seem to you, the clothes you wear set the scene for how people feel about not only you, but the office you work in and even the firm with which you are associated.

> Ted and Laura are buying a house and need a mortgage. They are nervous and apprehensive. This is the first time they have done anything like this and need to have someone to advise them properly. They go to their local bank. As they enter they see that the manager is busy with a client but there are two other bank employees in the mortgage department ready to speak with them. Both are young women in their mid-twenties, both smiling pleasantly—one dressed in a gray jacket and skirt and a blue blouse, the other in a beautiful ruffled chiffon dress in a peach pastel.
>
> The chances are great that Ted and Laura will head straight for the young woman in the gray jacket. Why? Because the first impression she puts forth inspires confidence in a bank setting. If the other young woman was working in a dance studio or hostessing a social event, she would inspire confidence there, but not in a bank.

BEING CHARMING

It is easy to be charming if you put your mind to it and be *truly* charming. By this we mean you cannot pretend. When you

CREATING A MORE ATTRACTIVE YOU

smile, you must really smile, when you listen you must be *hearing*, when you show concern, you must be *caring*. In other words, be sincere in what you are doing and saying. People see through insincerity very quickly.

Your eyes will give you away. The person who has a big beautiful smile but really is not interested in what you are saying will have a glazed or expressionless look in her eyes. Maintain eye contact with the other person while you are talking to her. This lets her know you are interested in what she is saying.

A HANDSHAKE IS IMPORTANT

Shaking hands is an everyday occurrence in business. People shake hands all the time: a visitor upon entering an office, two people meeting on the street, a person being introduced to another, people saying goodbye and so forth. The time was when it was only men who did the "handshaking," but now that women have entered the job market in large numbers, they have become "handshakers."

Women in business shake hands abiding by the same "unwritten rules" that men do. The handshake creates an impression that can be either positive or negative. The limp handshake shows you to be rather "wishy washy" or unsure of yourself, while the crushing grip indicates an overpowering, uncaring type of person. Use a *firm* handshake which conveys friendly, sincere interest and creates a very positive impression.

So assess yourself carefully. Think of ways you can be charming. They do not have to be the same ways used by someone else. Certain mannerisms may be charming when used by one person and ineffective when used by another. *You must be you,* and as *you,* you can be charming in your own special way.

> Margaret is rather shy and nervous when meeting new people. In her job as secretary to the manager of the purchasing department, she is called on to greet many vendors. Even though she is shy, she is able to cover up both her shyness and nervousness when meeting new people because her smile is sincere and her real interest in the callers and in her job is apparent.

IMPROVING YOUR VOICE AND DICTION

The tone of your voice and the clarity of your diction are very important. These things you can work on and improve yourself. Listen to others when you are speaking with them. Notice their diction. Observe how you are affected by their tone of voice or diction. Analyze your impressions of people and see what factors influence you most about them. Observe how others respond to you. Do people continually say "what?" to you when you talk to them or misunderstand what you are saying? Do they back off a little because your voice is too loud? As discussed in Chapter 6, try recording a conversation you are having with a friend and then listen and analyze it. You can tell if you are speaking too loudly, too softly, too quickly, or too slowly. You can also tell whether your diction is good and whether you sound polite, caring, and interested.

GOOD MANNERS ARE BASIC TO YOUR SUCCESS

Manners are a very important part of the total "you." We must "listen to ourselves" and be aware of others to see whether our manners are good, bad, or indifferent. Having good manners is not difficult, but often in our busy day, we forget to practice the manners that we know are right. The idea is to continually be aware of your manners so that good manners become a part of you and you do not have to "remember" to have good manners. When you are with friends, your manners may be a little more casual than they would be at work or when out socially. Generally, however it is a good idea to select a code of conduct that works and practice it all the time. Some people are more formal than others, some are more casual. You have to adopt a style that suits you. There are certain basic do's and don'ts that apply in all situations. The following checklist should help you.

1. Maintain eye contact with a person when you are speaking to him.
2. Do not neglect to make introductions and say the name of the older, more important person first.

CREATING A MORE ATTRACTIVE YOU

3. Show respect for visitors by standing as you greet them.
4. Do not interrupt people while they are talking.
5. Smoking may be allowed but be careful where you smoke. It may not be in your best interest to smoke at your desk or anywhere in the office except in the lounge or restroom. As you know, many people do not like to be near those who smoke. It is not unusual to see want ads in a newspaper for a secretary with good skills who does not smoke.
6. Chewing gum is considered inappropriate in a business office.
7. Walk around clusters of people talking—try not to go through them.
8. Avoid arguments or angry scenes in public.
9. Respect the privacy of others—especially your employer. There are times when people should not be interrupted unless it is an emergency.
10. Keep your voice low in public places. Whether you are in the office or a restaurant, avoid attracting undue attention to yourself.
11. Do not talk while chewing food. This is particularly difficult at business lunches where everyone is talking, but the rule still applies.
12. Use a firm handshake when appropriate as a greeting or during an introduction.

DRESSING FOR THE JOB

We all know that when we are looking for a job, we should dress with a suit or skirt and blouse or business dress. This is known as the coordinated look, which means that shoes, handbag, and stockings are also coordinated with whatever we are wearing to create a total look. After we get the job, we can then look around our offices and observe how others dress and we may be able to modify our style of clothing a little.

Employees of some companies, such as law firms, tend to dress more conservatively than others. A theatrical agency or recording company may be a little more liberal in their accepted attire, but most firms fall somewhere in the middle.

You may be doing everything else right in the office, but unless your grooming is appropriate, you will not be fully appreciated for the contributions you are making. For instance, observe the people in higher positions. See how they dress and notice things they do that promote good human relations. It is also good to take note of things they may be doing that do not promote good human relations.

Usually, those people who hold important positions in a company dress accordingly.

For the women: tailored suits, coordinated skirts and blouses, and tailored dresses. Choose colors that are becoming but that do not attract too much attention, such as brown, tan, blue, gray, and black. Color can be added attractively in blouses, sweaters, and scarves. Very pale pastels may not be appropriate for some offices. Remember to observe those around and above you and use good judgment in selecting your wardrobe.

For the men: Observe those men who hold executive or managerial positions and pattern your attire accordingly. Usually, business suits, shirts with ties in subdued colors are appropriate. Save sport and casual attire for leisure activities. Your choice of shoe style is also important in a business office.

Prepare for your job each week so that everything is in readiness which will in turn help you to be calm and relaxed when you arrive at work. In preparing yourself, think about what you will be doing during the next week so that you can plan your wardrobe accordingly. Advance planning will enable you to have your clothes in readiness—cleaned, pressed, mended, shoes repaired and polished, and outfits coordinated. This will add to the ease and confidence with which you deal with people.

You might want to make a chart such as the following to help you plan your activities and wardrobe for the week ahead.

FOR WOMEN, MAKEUP AND HAIR STYLES ARE IMPORTANT

Everything about your appearance is important and you must give a lot of thought to your makeup and your hair style. The important thing to remember is the simpler, the better.

CREATING A MORE ATTRACTIVE YOU 211

Makeup that is difficult to apply and has to be coordinated with every outfit is not for the office. Find several basic items of makeup that will go with everything and save the more exotic cosmetics for your leisure time activities.

There are many books and magazines that devote a lot of attention to the areas of being attractive. One book that is recommended is *Color Me Beautiful* by Carole Jackson (Ballantine, 1981). Investigate them, try out the ideas they give. Also, most cosmetic companies have brochures available that they will send to you on request. Another source of help is cosmetic

Chart for Planning Weeks Activities

	Monday	Tuesday	Wednesday	Thursday	Friday
Activities	Exec. Bd. Mtg Important Visitors from out of town		Lawyers meet w/ Boss Take Notes	Lunch w/ Fran	
Clothes	Grey Suit w/ light blue blouse black shoes	Plum Paisley w/ Black shoes	Brown Tweed suit w/ beige blouse brown shoes		
Have Ready	List of those attending Mtg. Min. of Pres. Mtg. Easel for presentation				

Figure 14-1

counters in department stores. They frequently have free makeup demonstrations for which you can sign up.

Experiment with hair styles until you find one that is practically "maintenance free." You cannot be combing, brushing, and fixing up your hair all day. Again, save the more involved styles for going out.

Above all, notice how the people in the positions above you look. They are your role models in your particular job.

FOR WOMEN—A CHECKLIST OF COMMON MAKEUP DON'TS

1. Extreme shades of lipstick should not be worn in the office.
2. Evening eye makeup, such as metallics and vivid hues, are out of place.
3. Chipped nail polish is worse then no polish.
4. Avoid extremes in cheek color and makeup shades. Your makeup should give your face a healthy glow.
5. Stockings that are too much of a contrast to what you are wearing are out of place. Instead choose neutral tones that blend with what you are wearing. You should not attract too much attention to your legs and feet.
6. Hair styles and color should not be extreme.

FOR WOMEN—A CHECKLIST OF WAYS TO ENHANCE YOUR APPEARANCE

1. Freshen makeup throughout the day as needed.
2. Keep fingernails neatly manicured and clean. If polish is worn, apply it as often as needed.
3. Seek advice on proper makeup from a specialist. (Advice from consultants is available in department stores and beauty salons, as well as in books and magazines).
4. Choose a hairstyle that suits the shape of your face and is _easy_ to care for.
5. Carry spare makeup for touch-up in your bag.
6. Leave an extra pair of stockings at the office.
7. Wear neat, comfortable shoes. (Attractive shoes can also be neat, comfortable, and appropriate for the office).

CREATING A MORE ATTRACTIVE YOU

8. Keep shoes clean and in good repair.
9. Check hemline before going out.

FOR MEN—A CHECKLIST OF WAYS TO ENHANCE YOUR APPEARANCE

1. Keep fingernails neatly trimmed and clean.
2. Hairstyles should be appropriate to business. (Hair, beard, and moustache should be well trimmed.)
3. Keep shoes shined and repaired.
4. Coordinate colors—suit, shirt, tie, socks, etc.
5. Have suits cleaned and pressed regularly.
6. Wear fresh shirts always (A wilted shirt even though it may be clean gives a poor impression.).

For more information on how to dress for the job, read John Molloy's books *Dress for Success* (Peter H. Wyden) 1975 and *The Women's Dress for Success Book* (Follett) 1977.

EATING THE RIGHT FOODS

A good diet is important. Follow a few basic nutrition guidelines.

1. Follow a well-balanced diet.
2. Eat and drink in moderation.
3. Remember that calories count.
4. Beware of fad diets.

To achieve a well-balanced diet, the guidelines as set forth by the U.S. Department of Health and Human Services suggests that we eat a variety from the four basic food groups (see figure 14-2).

It has been said "we are what we eat." If we don't eat properly, eventually our bodies will show it. It will become evident in the way we gain or lose weight, how alert we are and what our level of energy is.

Good nutrition means that all the essential foods are being eaten. One cannot maintain proper health unless this is an ongoing process along with adequate exercise.

214   **CREATING A MORE ATTRACTIVE YOU**

    A balanced diet that includes all the essential nutrients is necessary to maintain proper health and well being. The essentials include: carbohydrates, fats, protein, vitamins, minerals, and water.

    Beware of fasting and fad diets to control weight. Lack of, or inadequate amounts of, any of the essential nutrients will take their toll on the body. The effects may not be apparent right away but be assured they will show up.

    Don't take that risk. Good health is too important to be taken lightly. You will perform your job much more efficiently and effectively if your body is at its optimum.

WHAT ABOUT FAST FOODS?

    Today, with the fast paced life that most of us lead, we have to consciously think about nutrition and exercise, which are easy to put on the back burner. You are in a hurry to get from one meeting to another, or from work to an evening class, so you stop in at a fast food restaurant and get a calorie laden sandwich, french fries, and soft drink to hold you until you get home. Or you get so busy with your work that you forget to eat lunch and by 5 o'clock, you are so hungry that you get something quick, probably high calorie, and low in essential nutrients.

    This is not only a bad habit to fall into, but it establishes poor eating patterns and can lead to weight problems. If you

Figure 14-2

must on occasion eat on the run, you can, with a little advance planning, alter these patterns by carrying a nutritional snack with you. For instance, take fresh fruit, yogurt, whole grain bread and cheese, unsalted nuts and dried fruit, and so forth. In fact, you may not have to take it with you, because there are restaurants and take-out establishments where these types of foods are available. The choice is up to you.

EXERCISE FOR GOOD HEALTH

Proper exercise, which is essential to good health, enhances the body's performance and aids normal bodily functions such as digestion, metabolism, and elimination. It also strengthens blood vessels, and tones and strengthens muscle tissue. In order to be effective, proper exercise should become a regular part of your life. It should be something that is not too strenuous and that you enjoy, such as swimming, dancing, or walking. Whether you do it for recreation or strictly for the exercise, the main point to remember is that it should be regular, along with a nutritionally balanced diet.

GETTING PROPER REST

Few people can go without rest and still do a good job. What you do outside office hours affects how you conduct yourself while on the job. If you have not had enough sleep, you will probably be cranky and unfriendly. Things that ordinarily you can handle without any problem become major events in your day's work. Eight to ten hours sleep a night is still considered necessary for a person to be able to handle the activities of the remaining 14-16 hours. So budget your time accordingly.

SETTING ASIDE TIME FOR PLAY

In budgeting your time, you must make time for play, hobbies, studying—all the things that make you the special person that you are. You cannot only work and sleep—there is more to life than that and in order to do your job and be attractive both physically and mentally, you must make time for pursuing interests other than your job. Otherwise, you will begin to notice that people find you dull and uninteresting because you really have nothing to contribute. In turn, this will make you feel insecure about yourself. So think constructively and plan for the more attractive you.

AND DON'T FORGET...

Sensitive areas such as your weight, teeth, breath, personal hygiene are very important. Weight should be controlled because even though you have all the right clothes, they will not look as nice on an overweight person as they should. Teeth should be properly maintained. A beautiful smile is not as nice if it displays teeth that obviously need attention. Also, your breath and personal hygiene (including use of deodorants) are important in dealing with people. If you are not careful about these areas, you will offend others and your ability to communicate effectively will be hindered.

The secretary's success formula includes all of these elements. Each is important and each plays a major part in determining how well you function in your job. (See figure 14-3.)

PLANNING AND THINKING CONSTRUCTIVELY

There are many advantages to thinking and planning ahead. You will be able to organize your activities in your head, you can make notes about things that need to be taken care of in advance, and you can contact the people involved. Suppose you are hostessing an executive board meeting for your boss on Monday morning. If you have been thinking about it in advance and planning, you will approach that day with greater confidence and a feeling of well being, secure in the knowledge that things have been taken care of well in advance.

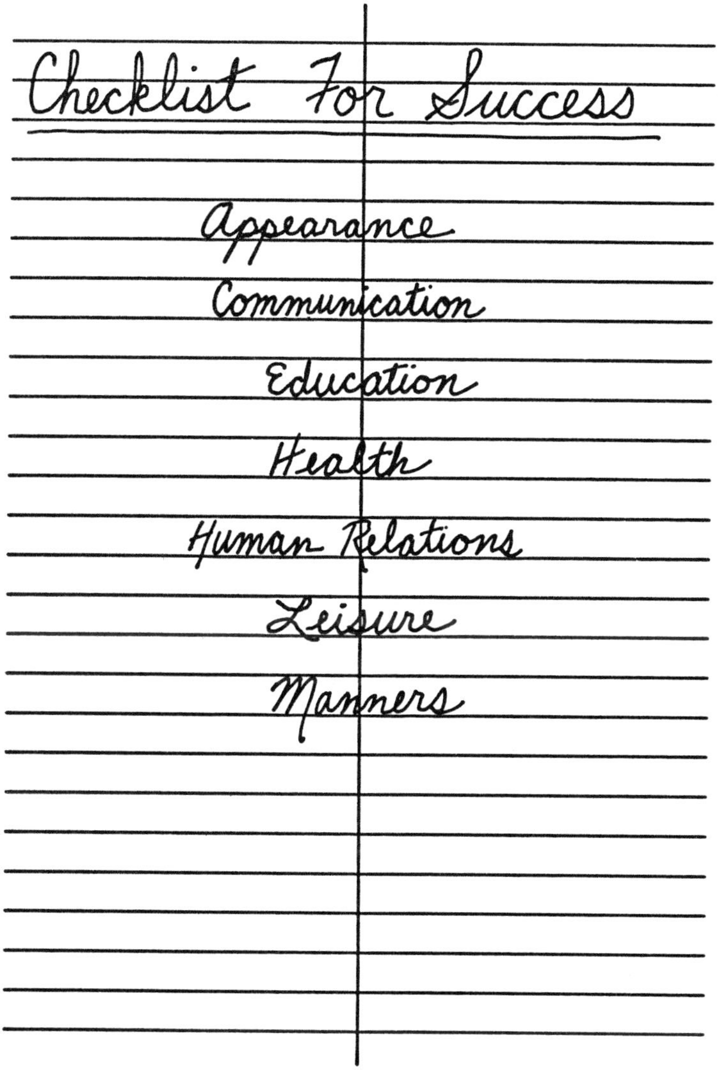

Checklist For Success

Appearance
Communication
Education
Health
Human Relations
Leisure
Manners

Figure 14-3

WRAPPING UP

"Creating a more attractive you" means that you are careful about every aspect of your personal appearance and conduct, and that you consciously try to do these things that promote good health and well being.

Help is available if you really want to improve your appearance. Books and magazines are a major source of reliable and helpful information. For instance, *Color Me Beautiful*, by Carole Jackson, is an excellent book for women that covers everything from makeup to color coordinating your wardrobe. For men *Dress for Success* by John Molloy is helpful. Also, *The Women's Dress for Success Book* by Molloy is a good source. There are many other books, magazines, and pamphlets available in bookstores, newsstands, and at your library.

Creating a more attractive you is an on-going process. You must continually work at it. The key word is "awareness." You must be aware of all that is going on around you and be willing to change and update to meet the particular sets of demands your job and social contacts require.

15

Achieving a Good Working Atmosphere

The total of what we have been discussing up to now could perhaps be made into a checklist for achieving a good working atmosphere and would include the following:

1. practicing good human relations
2. dealing effectively with everyone
3. handling stressful situations competently
4. helping to avoid conflicts
5. understanding scope of responsibility
6. exercising discretion
7. acting with tact and diplomacy
8. handling callers properly
9. communicating effectively both orally and in writing
10. having good telephone techniques
11. good management of office, social, and personal relationships

There are a few more items that we could include in our checklist:

12. providing a cooperative atmosphere
13. maintaining an attractive office
14. making the reception area "receptive"

These last three items are important because the working atmosphere is made up of the people *and* the office environment.

PROVIDING A COOPERATIVE ATMOSPHERE

A cooperative atmosphere includes many things—people feeling that they can work happily and productively in a particular situation.

This includes not only the people with whom you work and the supervisors, managers, and executives under whom you work, but the physical setting and the attitude of the clientele.

All of these factors can be influenced by the secretary. Along with care in handling interpersonal relationships and creating a receptive atmosphere, the attractiveness of the office helps to set the tone not only for the workers but for those who visit your office.

MAINTAINING AN ATTRACTIVE OFFICE

The first impression that the visitor has of a waiting room and reception area is extremely important. People form opinions very quickly, therefore it is imperative that the reception area be clean, neat, and attractive. It sets the stage and influences people positively or negatively in their contact with the company. It is especially important that a visitor's first visit creates a favorable impression.

Usually the design and decoration of the office is handled by professionals hired by the firm. However, under some circumstances such as a new company just getting started, you, as secretary, may be involved in the decorating, or, in your capacity as office manager, it may be left entirely up to you. If this is the case, you may want to call in a professional decorator (with your employer's approval) to help in the purchase of furnishings and in the decorating of the office. Because it is your responsibility to see that this is done properly, it is wise to get advice from experts trained in this field.

ACHIEVING A GOOD WORKING ATMOSPHERE

Keep in mind certain basic points reflecting good taste and the physical comfort and well being of the office personnel, such as the selection of a basic color scheme. Choose chairs that are attractive, comfortable, and durable, and colors that do not show soil and wear readily.

If you are responsible for selecting equipment and furniture, make sure that you talk to experts about the type of equipment, workstations, lighting, and so forth. These factors are becoming increasingly important considerations that affect the comfort and well being of the users of electronic equipment such as word processors.

MAKING THE RECEPTION AREA "RECEPTIVE"

The actual care and maintenance of this area may not be your responsibility in your role as secretary, but if you are a supervisor or office manager, it may be part of your job. For instance:

> If the President of the company is showing someone around, walks into your reception area, and finds dirty ashtrays or magazines scattered around, he may want to know who the supervisor is in that department. You are obviously not much of a *support* to your boss in this situation.

Your employer may have definite ideas as to how the office and reception area should look, and you must go along with these ideas. If, however, you feel that improvements could be made, discuss this with your employer and be ready to give reasons for your suggestions.

For instance:

> If the secretary's desk is not located where visitors are easily visible when they enter the reception area and you think that it could be located in a more convenient spot, you would want to suggest this change. But, before making your suggestion, list all the reasons and be careful how you approach your employer on this matter. Don't begin with something like, "Mr. Martin, you know the receptionist's desk is located in the *wrong* place. ... " Instead, it would be

better to introduce the subject tactfully by saying for example: "Mr. Martin, I was looking at the decorator's design for the reception area and I noticed that the receptionist desk seems to be in a spot where visitors might not be easily visible when they enter. Maybe it would be better if the desk were located on the other side. What do you think?"

If, however, you have a free hand in caring for, planning, and decorating the office, you may not have to ask approval or "sell" your boss on a new idea or suggestion. Nevertheless, you should send a memorandum to your employer concerning your ideas or suggestions.

Generally speaking, the reception area should be pleasant, restful, clean, neat, comfortable, and decorated appropriately for the type of business clientele that your company has.

Display current issues of magazines, depending on the interest of the clients and other visitors. Suitable magazines should be ordered. For example, magazines having to do with finances and accounting would be appropriate for an accounting firm.

If smoking is permitted, ashtrays should be easily accessible and clean. If smoking is not permitted, signs should be displayed clearly indicating this. Some firms prefer to have signs made up thanking people for not smoking rather than simply saying "No Smoking." Even if smoking is not allowed, have ashtrays for people to dispose of cigarettes if they are smoking as they enter.

Plants enhance the appearance of any office and especially the reception area. Remember, though, that in order for a plant to have a cheerful influence, it must be alive and thriving. If you do not have a "green thumb," another alternative is to employ a plant service that supplies and takes care of plants.

HOW TO HAVE AN UNCLUTTERED DESK

Whether the reception desk is separated from the reception area by a partition or is immediately visible, the desk and area around it should be kept in an orderly condition. Even if the desk is behind a partition, special care should be taken to see that clutter does not accumulate.

Some offices have more paper work than others. These may be stacks of files, returns from duplicating, and so forth. Take care to have papers filed and cleared off each day before leaving; don't allow things to accumulate. This is sometimes difficult and as it is important that records and files be kept up to date, you must make sure to arrange the time to do this. You may need a part-time clerical person. Evaluate the needs of your firm and your boss, and work out a solution that is agreeable to both you and your employer. Remember that in the end it is your responsibility to find a solution.

OFFICE APPEARANCE IS IMPORTANT

The general appearance of the office must be neat; the chairs should be arranged so that visitors are easily seen from the receptionist's desk, wall pictures should be straight, and draperies or blinds neatly arranged.

Your employer's desk is of equal importance. Help keep it cleared of excess material every day. The impression a visitor gets looking over a stack of papers at your employer or when your boss has to fumble through papers looking for some information is very poor. The feeling created is a negative one—that the executive is disorganized and may not be reliable. In addition, the impression given of the company may be a negative one.

PRACTICING GOOD HUMAN RELATIONS

The practice of good human relations must become part of your personality. It must be natural. You cannot say, "O.K. now I must practice good human relations." You will not always do the right thing and you will sometimes lose your temper or your "cool," but that is not cause to give up. You must keep striving. Some points to remember are:

1. You can only control how *you* act and respond, not how someone else does.

2. If you are polite and considerate when dealing with people, the chances are they will respond in kind. If you are impolite and inconsiderate, the chances are people will treat you that way.

3. However, a sharp remark or impolite behavior directed *at* you should not invoke that kind of response *from* you.

4. You must maintain "cool control" of each situation.

5. React positively not negatively in situations; always think of a positive, constructive outcome to a situation, not a negative, destructive one.

DEALING EFFECTIVELY WITH EVERYONE

Dealing effectively with everyone is an enormous challenge, but it can be done (most of the time) if you don't react negatively to the other person.

For example:

> The parking lot attendant at the facility where Teresa works is very grumpy. Often when she arrives he is waving people off and telling them to go down to the next lot because his is full. She knows there is probably a spot there and at any rate many people will soon be leaving as it is close to a shift change when she arrives. She sees people arguing with him and getting nowhere. Every morning she drives up and says, "Good Morning" to him with a smile—when he tells her to go the next lot, she says, "Oh how I wish I could get in here—well maybe I'll be luckier tomorrow—Have a good day." After a few days of this she arrives one morning expecting him to do the same thing and he motions her on, opens the gate and says, "If you wait a few minutes you'll get a spot." She thanks him and from then on has no problem.

HANDLING STRESSFUL SITUATIONS COMPETENTLY

Stress is something we hear more and more about every day, there are books written about it, practically every newspaper or magazine we read has something to say about stress, how it affects our health, how it affects our general well being, and how it affects our performance on the job.

As secretary to an executive in a key position, you deal with all kinds of situations and must expect to be under some stress. You cannot expect things to run smoothly all of the time. You can play an important role in assuming some of the routine tasks that tend to fragment and frustrate your boss. By anticipating problems before they actually materialize, you can shoulder some of your employer's headaches and free him or her for other responsibilities.

This is no small task; it takes a creative, intelligent person, skilled in the art of dealing with people. It also involves exercising judgment, creativeness, and high-level decision-making skills. Even though your job description may not spell out every task in detail, your scope of responsibility necessarily covers a broad range of activities that can become stressful at times.

SOME CAUSES OF STRESS

1. repetitive work that seems endless
2. glare from poor lighting
3. chairs and desks that are not proper height for maximum comfort and efficiency
4. temperature that is either too hot or too cold
5. boss venting personal anger and frustrations on you, just because you are available
6. possessing knowledge without the authority to act—a secretary often possesses knowledge of and is involved in important operations of the business but lacks the opportunity or the authority to actually make decisions and implement actions.
7. poor career advancement opportunity
8. low pay in some instances
9. married women who carry a heavy load both at the office and at home
10. single parents who have the responsibility of rearing children

11. poor diet
12. lack of physical exercise

CHECKLIST ON HOW TO DEAL WITH STRESS

1. Talk out your problem.
2. Get away from the source of the pressure even if it is only for a cup of coffee or lunch.
3. Exercise such as walking, swimming, calisthenics, or even rearranging your desk, helps to relieve stress.
4. Don't allow yourself to be hindered from doing anything when you run into a problem. Go on to something else and forget about your problem for a while. When you come back to it later, you will bring fresh insight and renewed effort.
5. Don't dwell on mistakes or missed goals. Look at your accomplishments and move on from there.
6. Sometimes it is better to give in than to fight over something that may not be all that important.
7. Leave your job at the office.
8. Soak in a hot tub or sit in a sauna.
9. Find a hobby or activity that you enjoy and that involves you so completely that you forget about your troubles.
10. Take a vacation even if it is only a short one. Get away from your usual routine.

HELPING TO AVOID CONFLICTS

Many of the situations we find ourselves in in our daily lives are potential conflict situations. Most conflicts can be avoided. Some conflict situations, of course, cannot be avoided, but they do not have to result in anger situations. That is the important thing to remember—if there is conflict, try to control it if you cannot avoid it completely:

> Anita and Cynthia are making plans for a department outing. Anita wants to go on a boat ride and Cynthia wants a picnic. Both women have worked very hard getting commitments on prices, dates, and food from the proprietors involved. In fact, Anita had to do a lot of practic-

ing of good human relations to get the boat owner to agree to the terms she wanted and Cynthia has gotten promises from the managers of the picnic area to provide lunch and games at a greatly reduced cost.

Now they come to each other with the plans. Of course, we all know they should have talked this through a bit more before they got so involved, but there had been a misunderstanding and each had thought she could make these commitments without the other's approval. They are both angry and upset about this. Dorothea, another secretary, suggests that they not worry about what should have been done but prepare a proposal including a sign-up sheet, for both trips, with the costs, and see what the response from the employees would be. In this way the conflict, though not avoided because both Anita and Cynthia want to have their own proposals accepted, is resolved positively and the employees will decide. Perhaps there will be two trips.

Another example of a stressful situation that you probably have encountered is:

Doreen's employer has been away for a week on a business trip. It is 9 A.M. Monday morning, and he is at his desk trying to get caught up on what has happened during the time he was away and also prepare for a 10 A.M. meeting with his superior.

He is nervous and is pressuring Doreen for various things. He is not being polite; in fact, he is acting as if Doreen is responsible for materials that cannot be located, but that he actually had on the trip with him.

Doreen is getting more and more upset and is afraid that either she will cry or will say something for which she will be sorry.

She suddenly decides what to do. She says to her boss, "Excuse me, I'll be right back, I'm not feeling too well, I must go to the rest room for a few minutes."

She got away from the situation for a few minutes and gave her employer a chance to realize that he was putting too much pressure on her because of his own feelings. In turn, she gave herself enough time to calm down so that she could deal with the situation, because she realized that he was only acting this way because of his stresses.

UNDERSTANDING THE SCOPE OF RESPONSIBIILITY

It is very important to realize where your job begins and where it ends, and, also, where your boss's job begins and ends—in other words, the "scope of responsibility." You are an aid and support to your boss—you are not the boss—and your employer depends on you greatly. You become accustomed to anticipating his decisions on matters, but you must always be aware of the difference between situations in which you can use your initiative and make the decision, and situations in which you may be stepping over the line and usurping your employer's authority.

All situations are different and you must decide, on your own, exactly at what point you would be "stepping over the line."

For example:

> Inez is secretary to the Manager of the Purchasing Department. They have ordered thirty electronic typewriters for various departments in the company. Inez receives a telephone call from the typewriter company saying that the price has been raised on the typewriters that they ordered, but if they will accept a different model, they can get the same price if they act immediately. Inez checks this model and discovers that it has most of the capabilities of the model ordered so she agrees. It does not, however, come in the colors desired.

Unless her employer has specifically given her this authority, she has gone beyond her scope of authority. She should have gotten all the details as she did and made a decision, but indicated that she had to check with her employer although she felt sure it would be all right.

The Purchasing Manager was purchasing for various departments in the company, and the people involved might have specific requests for certain colors or capabilities. The Manager would have had to take full responsibility for any problems that had occurred. So Inez was not assisting and supporting her employer when she made this decision without approval.

EXERCISING DISCRETION

As a secretary, you may have all kinds of confidential information concerning your employer's business and private life. You are often in a position where you may be asked questions that you know the answers to but where you must exercise a great deal of discretion.

> Luanne's employer is in the process of getting a divorce. Members of the family are calling trying to get information of one sort or another, which Luanne suspects has to do with the divorce proceedings. Luanne is very uncomfortable because often she knows the answer but is not sure whether or not she should give it. She has decided to indicate that she does not know but she will certainly inquire of her boss and either call back herself or have her employer return the call. Often this results in the caller saying, "Never mind, I'll call myself later."

You, as a secretary, know that there are always situations in which you exercise discretion and, of course, if you always think in terms of your role as administrative *support* and *assistant,* you will keep the situation in the right perspective.

ACTING WITH TACT AND DIPLOMACY

Practically all of your dealings with people involve tact and diplomacy, whether it is in your business life or your personal life. How often has someone asked you, "How do you like my new haircut?" Have you ever replied, "I hate it, it's awful"? Probably not. If you don't like it you might say something like—"Oh, it makes you look so different; I'm so used to it the other way," or, "I didn't realize you had planned to have this style, it's very popular."

You are acting with tact and diplomacy. Had the person asked for your advice before the hair was cut you might have given it, but now you certainly would not deliberately hurt the person.

> Marina has two important clients come in to the Art Gallery at the same time to see her employer. If she shows

one in before the other it may be insulting and the client's business may be lost. Instead she brings out a portfolio that her employer wants one client to look at before they meet. Meanwhile, the other client will go in to see the employer. That way they will not waste any of the valuable time of either client, and neither will feel that he or she is getting preferential treatment.

HANDLING CALLERS PROPERLY

As you know, the receptionist duties that a secretary has are very important. Whether or not your firm has a receptionist, you will be receiving callers that come to see your employer. Sometimes people may come to see your employer without an appointment. This can be a difficult situation because the caller may be one that your employer wants to see, but cannot do so just then because of other appointments. You can say something to the effect that "Mr. Johnson is anxious to talk with you, but he is booked solid with appointments for the next two hours. Is there any way you can come back then, or could we make another appointment at your convenience."

The caller could be your boss's superior and you have a sensitive situation. If your employer leaves others waiting while he sees the superior, the superior may think that is an inappropriate practice.

You, as secretary, probably would say something like, "Mrs. Mendez is with a client right now. I'll ask her to step out for a few minutes." Unless it is terribly urgent, your employer's superior will probably either wait or come back or tell you what was wanted. In any event, you should let your employer know about the situation.

COMMUNICATING EFFECTIVELY BOTH ORALLY AND IN WRITING

One of the main things to remember when you are communicating with others is that there is a sender, a message, and a receiver. You are interested in getting your message to the receiver. You cannot leave things to chance, you must be

ACHIEVING A GOOD WORKING ATMOSPHERE

sure that the message you are sending is the one that is being received. Often we know what we mean by something we say but the other person receives an entirely different message.

For example:

> Veronica was not feeling well one morning. She called the office and left a message for her employer that she would not be in that day.
>
> She told the receptionist who answered the telephone that she had an upset stomach. She had been at a family anniversary party the night before, and she must have eaten something that disagreed with her because she was up all night.
>
> The receptionist left a note for Veronica's employer saying "Veronica called—she will not be in today, as she is not feeling well because she was out late last night."

Veronica was rather embarrassed when she came in the next day and her employer suggested she might be "partying" too much.

In this case the message sent was not the one received and the meaning was changed.

ADDING TO YOUR TELEPHONE SKILLS

So much business is accomplished over the telephone that it is essential that you employ the best telephone techniques possible. It is often difficult to deal with people over the telephone because they are not making eye contact with you and it is easy for a caller to get angry and say more than he might say if you were face-to-face.

For example:

> A caller wants to speak with your employer, who is not in at the moment. The caller gets very angry and demands to know where your boss is and why he is never available. You are even accused of not putting the call through.
>
> It is difficult to remain calm in this kind of a situation, but you cannot respond by getting angry. You must try to assure the caller that you will see that your employer gets the message and apologize for the inconvenience.

GOOD MANAGEMENT OF OFFICE SOCIAL AND PERSONAL RELATIONSHIPS

It is very important for you, as a secretary, to take care in managing office social and personal relationships. A big part of your life is spent on the job and, naturally, your relationships are not all of a business nature.

There are many opportunities to enter into social situations, but be careful that when attending an office social function such as an employee picnic or retirement dinner you still follow a behavior pattern that does not cause you embarrassment when you return to the office.

Also, even though you make close personal friends at your job, establish a policy at the beginning to separate your business and social life as much as possible. Even though one of your closest friends is a co-worker, it is not a good idea to "talk shop" away from the office. The less you discuss the office, the less chance there is for either of you to divulge information of a confidential nature, which can only harm both your friendship and your jobs.

BUT WHAT ABOUT YOU?

As we see, achieving a good working atmosphere is a composite of many factors. One that is very important and that cannot be forgotten is your own personal feeling about your job. You may do all the right things to help achieve this atmosphere, but for some reason things are not working out as well as you would like. Stop and think for a minute. If you are not happy yourself with your situation, no matter how hard you try to practice good human relations and achieve a good working atmosphere, you will not be successful.

Perhaps you may want to stop and ask yourself a few questions that may help you to see whether you need to reevaluate your own situation.

1. Am I always tired and bored?
2. Do I look forward to my evenings or weekends or vacations?

3. When co-workers discuss their leisure activities, do I just sit quietly and listen, never entering into the conversation?
4. Do I feel as if I need a change of pace?
5. Is my job becoming stressful?
6. Do I feel inferior when subjects are discussed that I know very little about?
7. Has my career hit a standstill?

If you are always tired and bored, do not look forward to free time, and never enter into conversation with co-workers, you probably need a change of pace. If you feel inferior when subjects are discussed that you know little about—perhaps you should learn something about them. Take a course, read a book, ask a friend—do not allow yourself to feel inferior. Perhaps your job has become too stressful or your career has hit a standstill. Analyze yourself, your job, and your social relationships objectively. You should find solutions to problems and this will help you do so.

WRAPPING UP

Dealing with people is something we all do all the time. Unless you live the existence of a hermit, you cannot escape "dealing with people." Whether you do it effectively or not is largely up to you. In your personal life, if you do not practice good human relations, the result will probably be that you spend a good deal of time being angry, annoyed and, probably, *alone.*

As a secretary, if you do not know how to deal effectively with people, you will probably not succeed in your job and will continually wonder why, with your good skills and education, you are either standing still or moving backward while others move beyond you.

Index

A

Acceptance, how to gain, 203-204
Advertisements and circulars,
   handling of, 100
American Association of Medical
   Assistants, 194
Appearance, office, 223
Appearance, personal, 32, 194:
   body language and, 108-110, 205
   checklist for, 216, 217
   checklist for men on ways to
      enhance, 213
   checklist for women on ways to
      enhance, 212-213
   diet and, 213-215
   exercise and, 215
   importance of clothing, 194, 206
      209-210
   importance of posture, 108, 205
   makeup and hairstyles, 210-212
   proper rest and, 215
   reactions from others toward your,
      205
   sources of information on, 211-212,
      213
   voice and diction and, 208
Appointments:
   handling visitors who do not have,
      43, 230
   how to avoid conflicts in scheduling,
      36-37, 39
   how to avoid unkept, 162
   use of catch-up time, 42

Assertiveness:
   being assertive with bosses, 128-129
   checklist for dealing assertively with
      problem situations, 201-202
   importance of, 25-26
Assistants, importance of
   interpersonal relationships with,
   149-151
Associates:
   being courteous with business,
      191-192
   socializing with business, 169
Atmosphere, good working:
   checklist for creating a, 200-201,
      219-220
   checklist for developing a positive,
      140-141
   creating a, with bosses, 113
   dealing effectively with everyone
      and, 224
   design of reception areas, 30, 31-32,
      220-222
   handling conflict and, 226-227
   handling stress and, 224-226
   how to creative a receptive, 30-32
   how to have an uncluttered desk,
      222-223
   importance of office appearance,
      223
   maintaining an attractive office,
      220-221
   practicing good human relations
      and, 223-224

Authoritarian leadership, 7
Authority, lines of, 145-147, 149-150:
   importance of informing staff, 150
   "gray areas" of, clearing up, 146-147, 149-150
   knowing your scope of, 228
   organization charts and, 146
   overall knowledge and, 150
   understanding what co-workers need, 150-151

B

Bills and statements, handling of, 100
Body language, oral communication and, 108-110, 205
Boss, preparing a:
   basic checklist for, 123-124
   checklist for, for a presentation, 124
   checklist for, for a trip, 124-125
Bosses:
   accepting gifts from, 186-187
   being assertive with, 128-129
   businesslike relations with, 195-196
   checklist for getting along with difficult, 198
   checklist for improving communication between secretaries and, 189
   coping with difficult situations with, 127-128
   creating the proper working atmosphere with, 113
   discussing problems with, 126-127
   getting along with, 189-190
   handling multiple, 114-116, 202, 203
   importance of compromise with, 120-121
   importance of teamwork with, 119, 126
   personal problems of, 189
   socializing with, 168-169, 195-196
   socializing with the spouses of, 169
   understanding, 121-123
   working with women, 117, 119-120, 197-198
   see also Liaison
Buddy system for secretaries, xviii
Business and Professional Women's Club, The, 194

Businesslike relations, keeping, 194-196
   checklist for maintaining, 196

C

Caller(s):
   checklist for handling the forgotten, 39, 41
   proper handling of, 230
Career objectives, defining, 10-11
Catch-up time, use of, 42
Charming, being, 206-207
Checklist(s):
   for avoiding conflict, 37, 38
   basic, for bosses, 123-124
   of common makeup don'ts, 212
   for creating a good working atmosphere, 200-201, 219-220
   for dealing assertively with problem situations, 201-202
   for dealing with difficult situations, 192
   for developing a positive atmosphere, 140-141
   for diplomacy in handling visitors, 47-49
   of duties, 18
   for getting along with a difficult boss, 198
   on good manners, 208-209
   for handling mail, 101
   for handling the forgotten caller, 39
   to help your boss prepare for a presentation, 124
   for housekeeping duties, 16, 17, 155
   on how to deal with stress, 226
   on how to get your boss ready for a trip, 124-125
   on how to motivate the people you supervise, 138
   for improving communication between the secretary and the boss, 189
   for improving leadership skills, 8, 9
   for improving your ability to speak and discuss, 110-111
   for improving your effectiveness on the telephone, 57-58, 163
   for increasing efficiency, 154-155

INDEX

Checklist(s) *(cont'd)*
  for maintaining businesslike relationships, 196
  for maintaining open lines of communication, 193
  for men on ways to enhance appearance, 213
  for overcoming barriers to communication, 137
  for planning office parties, 181-182
  for preventing a crisis, 199-200
  of secretarial duties, 154-155
  for the secretary as liaison for the boss, 141
  for selecting stationery, 92, 93-95
  of services, 155
  for setting priorities, 154
  for solving problems, xvi
  for starting a new club or program, 183
  for success, 216, 217
  for supervising other employees, 136-137
  of supplies and equipment, 155
  of telephone reminders, 64
  for traveling, 174-176
  use of, 16, 18
  use of, to increase efficiency, 154-156
  for women on ways to enhance appearance, 212-213
Classes, participating in, 182-183
Clothing:
  importance of, 194, 206, 209-210
  for men, 210
  for women, 210
Club(s):
  checklist for starting a new program or, 183
  participating in company, 182-183
Colleagues:
  cooperating with, 193
  keeping up to date with, 192-194
Color Me Beautiful, 211
Communictions. *see* Oral communication; Written communications
Compromise, importance of, 120-121
Confidences, discussion of business, 170, 179, 229

Conflict:
  checklist for avoiding, 37, 38
  how to handle, 226-227
  human relations and avoiding, 163-164
  in scheduling appointments, 36-37, 39
Congratulations letter, example of, 90
Cooperating:
  with colleagues, 193
  with co-workers, 190-191, 202, 203
Copability profile, 11-12
Cosmetics and hairstyles, 210-212
Courteous, importance of being, 191-192
Cover letter, examples of, 84-85
Co-workers:
  checklist for motivating, 138
  cooperating with, 190-191, 202, 203
  dealing with mature, 198-199
  how to handle, 196-197
  supervising, 143
  understanding the needs of, 150-151
Crises, dealing effectively with, 199-200
Customers and clients:
  being courteous to, 191-192
  socializing with, 180

D

Deadlines, setting realistic, 151
Decision making, guide for, 25
Delegating tasks, how to do, 18-19
Democratic leadership, 7, 148
Desk, how to have an uncluttered, 222-223
Dictatorial leadership, 147-148
Diction, improving, 208
Diet, importance of, 213-215
Diplomacy:
  checklist for, in handling visitors, 47-49
  using tact and, 229-230
Discretion, need for, 229
Discussion of business confidences, 170, 179
Discussion skills, tips for improving, 110-111

Dress:
 importance of, 194, 206, 209-210
 for men, 210
 for women, 210
Dress for Success, 213
Duties:
 checklist of, 18
 checklist of secretarial duties, 154-155

E

Efficiency, use of checklists to increase, 57-58, 154-155
Emotions, importance of controlling, 20
Equipment, checklist of, 155
Exercise, importance of, 215

F

Fast foods, problem with, 214-215
Favorites, playing, 191-192
First impressions, importance of, 103-104, 206
Free time, guidelines for planning, 173, 176
Friends:
 choosing, 171-172
 socializing with, 170

G

Gifts:
 accepting, 186-187
 handling collections for, 183, 186
Goal setting:
 importance of, 8, 10
 realistic, 151
 time management and, 152-153
Good will, how to spread, 159-160
Gossip, dealing with, 170
Grammar skills, improving:
 comma usage, 76-78
 quotation marks, use of, 80-81
 spelling and word division, 78-80
"Gray areas" of supervision, clearing up, 146-147, 149-150

H

Hairstyles, makeup and, 210-212
Handshake, importance of the, 207

Housekeeping duties, checklists for, 16, 17, 155
Human relations:
 avoiding conflicts, 163-164
 businesslike, 194-196
 dealing effectively with everyone, 224
 dealing with rudeness and verbal abuse, 158
 description of, 157
 good, on the telephone, 52
 guidelines for practicing good, 223-224
 handling stressful situations, 224-226
 how to avoid unkept appointments, 162
 how to deal with disgruntled callers, xv, xvii-xviii
 how to spread good will, 159-160
 improving, through oral communication, 105
 need for discretion, 229
 role of secretary in, 157-159
 screening of telephone calls, 162-163
 tips on dealing with the unexpected, 33, 40, 42, 161-162
 tips on greeting visitors, 160-161
 using tact, and diplomacy, 229-230

I

Image:
 how a caller views you, xiv
 importance of first impressions, 103-104, 206
 personal appearance, 32, 194
 reflections on a company, xiii
 role of secretary in projecting a good, 157-159
 steps to take to improve organization, xiv-xv
Impressions, importance of first, 103-104, 206
Information letter, example of, 86
Informing staff, authority and importance of, 150
Innovation, importance of, 21, 25
Insincerity:
 greeting people and, 206-207
 supervising and, 151

INDEX

Interpersonal relationships with assistants, importance of, 149-151

J

Jackson, Carole, 211
Januz, Lauren Robert, 153
Job descriptions:
  need for, 14
  supervising and use of, 143-144
Jones, Susan K., 153

K

Kidding, problem with, 194
Knowledge, authority and overall, 150

L

Laissez-faire leadership, 7, 148
Lakin, Alan, 10
Leadership:
  checklist for improving leadership skills, 8, 9
  essentials of effective, 8
  factors that influence, 7-8
  how to improve one's skills of, 8
  types of, 7, 147-148
Leisure activities, key factors in planning, 176-177
Letters. *see* Written communications
Liaison:
  between bosses and customers, 133-134, 139-140
  between bosses and other employees, 196-197
  between bosses and secretaries, 130-131
  checklist for the secretary as liaison for the boss, 141
  definition of, 130
  example of making your boss look good, 131-132
  how to get a message across, 132-133
  how to increase your effectiveness in the area of, 140-141
  importance of respect, 135-136
  personal characteristics necessary to maintain a successful, 130
  smoothing the way between your boss and your boss's superior, 131
  tips for successful, with those you supervise, 136-138

Liason *(cont'd)*
  with maintenance people, 138-139
  with superiors, 189-190
Listening skills:
  how to improve, 57, 107
  inhibitors to good, 107

M

Magazines, display of, 222
Mail:
  advertisements and circulars, 100
  bills and statements, 100
  checklist for handling, 101
  handling the contents, 99-100
  periodicals and professional publications, 101
  personal, 100
  processing of incoming, 98-99
  professional, 100
  sorting of, 99
  what to do with, when the boss is away, 101-102
Maintenance people, getting along with, 138-139
Makeup and hairstyles, 210-212
Managing, how to improve:
  acceptance of change and, 20-21
  assertiveness and, 25-26
  controlling emotions, 20
  decision making and, 25
  delegating tasks and, 18-19
  importance of being organized, 14-16
  innovation and, 21, 25
  supervising effectively, 19-20
  use of check lists for, 16, 18
  use of job descriptions for, 14
  see also Supervising
Management theory, 147-149
Manners, checklist for good, 208-209
Men:
  checklist for, on ways to enhance appearance, 213
  clothing for, 210
Messages:
  how to get a message across, 132-133
  how to take telephone, 58-59, 61-62
Molloy, John, 213
Motivating co-workers:
  checklist for, 138
  supervising and, 143

N

Name recognition, importance of, 62-63
National Association of Bank Women, Inc., 194
National Association of Education Secretaries, 194
National Association of Legal Secretaries, 194

O

Office:
  importance of the appearance of the, 223
  maintaining an attractive, 220-221
Office parties planning of, 180-182
Office social life. *see* Social life, in the office
Oral communication:
  body language and, 108-110
  checklist for improving, 110-111
  checklist for improving communication between the secretary and the boss, 189
  checklist for maintaining open lines of, 193
  checklist for overcoming barriers to, 137
  dealing with speech problems, 47
  importance of first impressions, 103-104
  importance of listening, 107
  improving human relations skills through, 105
  smiling and, 104
  tips for effective, 104, 230-231
  tone of your voice and, 104, 106
  use of videotaping to improve, 109
  volume of your voice and, 104, 106
Organization:
  chart, use of an, 146, 147
  importance of having good, 14-16
  steps to take to improve, xiv-xv
  use of checklists and, 16, 18
Organizations, types of secretarial, 194

P

Paternalistic leadership, 148
Periodicals, display of, 222
Periodicals and professional publications, handling of, 101
Personal appearance. *see* Appearance, personal
Personality traits:
  ambitious, 3
  how to adjust one's behavior, 6
  how to do a profile of your, 4-6
  identifying one's, 1-2
  a "late-starter," 2-3
  list of, 4
  a "morning" person, 2
  perfectionist, 3-4
  social interaction and developing, 177
Personal mail, handling of, 100
Personal problems, listening to, 189
Physical layouts, effects of, on supervising, 151-152
Planning and thinking constructively, 216
Posture, oral communication and, 108, 205
Presentation, checklist to help your boss prepare for a, 124
Pressure, handling, 40
  see also Stress
Priorities, setting, 153-154
Professional mail, handling of, 100, 101
Professional organizations, membership in:
  keeping up to date through, 192-194
  similar problems met by, 8
  types of secretarial, 194
Professional Secretaries International (PSI), 113, 194
Progress charts, supervising and, 151
PSI (Professional Secretaries International), 113, 194
Public, dealing with the. *see* Human relations

R

"Rate Yourself Chart," 4
Reception areas, design of, 30, 31-32, 220-222
Receptionist, role as a:
  advice on handling all types of visitors, 44-46

INDEX

Receptionist, role as a *(cont'd)*
  checklist for diplomacy in handling visitors, 47-49
  guidelines for being an effective, 28
  first impressions, 33, 35-36
  handling pressure, 40
  handling unexpected situations, 33, 40, 42, 161-162
  handling visitors who do not have appointments, 43, 230
  how to create a receptive atmosphere, 30-32
  keeping notes on visitors, 28-29, 33, 35
  making everyone feel special, 42-44
  personal appearance, 32
  physical layout of the area and, 30, 31-32
  proper handling of visitors, 230
  scheduling appointments, 36-37, 39
  tips for screening visitors, 44
  tone of voice when dealing with visitors, 29, 46-47
  ways to increase your effectiveness as a, 46-49
Recreation. *see* Social relationships
Relatives, socializing with, 171
Reprimanding workers, 151
Request letter, examples of, 87-88
Respect, importance of, 135-136
Responsibility, knowing your scope of, 228
Rest, importance of proper, 215
Rudeness and verbal abuse, dealing with, 158

S

Schedules, vacation, 174, 175
Scheduling appointments:
  how to avoid conflicts, 36-37, 39
  use of catch-up time, 42
Screening:
  of telephone calls, 53, 162-163
  of visitors, 44
Secretarial duties, checklist of, 154-155
Secretarial organizations, types of, 194
Secretary, definition of, 113
Secretary/office supervisor, duties of, 145-146
Self, knowledge of, 1-12

Services, checklist of, 155
Sexual harrassment, 195-196
Smiling, importance of, 104
Social activities:
  choosing, 172-173
  participating in group activities, 182-183
  setting time for, 215-216
  whether married or single, 176
Social life, in the office:
  accepting gifts, 186-187
  balance between work and, 178-179
  discussion of business confidences, 179
  handling collections for gifts, 183, 186
  participating in group activities, 182-183
  planning office parties, 180-182
  with customers and clients, 180
Social relationships:
  balance between work and, 167, 232
  checklists for traveling, 174-176
  choosing friends, 171-172
  developing personality traits and, 177
  guidelines for planning free time, 173, 176
  importance of, 167-168
  key factors in planning leisure activities, 176-177
  managing vacation time, 173-174
  with the boss, 168-169, 195-196
  with the boss's spouse, 169
  with business associates, 169
  with friends, 170
  with relatives, 171
Solving problems, checklist for, xvi
Speaking, checklist for improving your ability of, 110-111
"Special Occasion Fund," 186
Speech:
  dealing with speech problems, 47
  improving your, 208
Stationery:
  checklist for selecting, 92, 93-95
  how to choose, 92
  quality of, 92, 98
Stress:
  causes of, 225-226
  checklist on how to deal with, 226
Subordinate-centered leadership, 7

Success:
  achieving, through goal setting, 8, 10-11
  checklist for, 216, 217
Superiors, getting along with, 189-190
Supervising:
  checklist for, other employees, 136-137, 138
  checklists for improving your efficiency, 154-155
  clearing up "gray areas," 146-147, 149-150
  effectively, 19-20
  effects of physical layout on, 151-152
  importance of informing staff, 150
  importance of interpersonal relationships, 149-151
  insincerity and, 151
  key factors for success in, 156
  lines of authority and, 145-147, 149-150
  management theory and, 147-149
  motivating the staff and, 143
  overall knowledge and, 150
  progress charts and, 151
  setting priorities, 153-154
  setting realistic time limits and deadlines, 151
  reprimanding workers, 151
  time management and, 152-153
  understanding what co-workers need, 150-151
  use of an organization chart, 146, 147
  use of job description, 143-144
  see also Managing, how to improve
Supplies, checklist of, 155

T

Tact and diplomacy, using, 229-230
Tasks:
  how to delegate, 18-19
  keeping records of, 21, 25
  time management and, 152-153
Teams, participating in company, 182-183
Teamwork, importance of, 119, 126
Telephone, effective use of the:
  angry callers, dealing with, 63-64, 231
  answering calls for others, 54

Telephone, effective use of the *(cont'd)*
  checklist for improving your effectiveness on the, 57-58, 163
  checklist of telephone reminders, 64
  expressions and tone of voice used, 50-51
  good human relations on the, 52
  handling of multiple calls, 58
  how to answer the, 51-52
  how to get the caller to talk, 55-57
  how to place calls, 53-54
  improving your listening skills, 57
  improving your voice, diction, and manner, 68-69
  maintaining control on the, 64
  messages, how to take, 58-59, 61-62
  providing coverage of the, when you are absent, 65-66
  revealing too much information on the, 64-65
  screening calls, 53, 162-163
  seminars for employees on proper usage of the, 66-68
  tips on handling the, 55, 68-69
  use of names on the, 62-63
Thank you letter, example of, 89
Theory X, 149
Theory Y, 149
Tickler file, use of, 153
Time limits, setting realistic, 151
Time management, 152-153
Time Management for Executives, 153
Tone of voice:
  improving the, 208
  oral communication and, 104, 106
  on the telephone, 50-51, 68-69
  when dealing with visitors, 29, 46-47
Transmittal letter, example of, 84
Traveling:
  checklists for, 174-176
  checklist to help your boss prepare for, 124-125

U

Unexpected situations:
  dealing effectively with crises, 199-200
  examples of, 202-203
  handling, 33, 40, 42, 161-162
  patience needed in, 40, 42
  tips on dealing with, 161-162

INDEX

V

Vacation time, managing, 173-174
Verbal abuse and rudeness, dealing with, 158
Videotapes, improving oral communication by using, 109
Visitor(s):
  advice on handling all types of, 44-46
  checklist for diplomacy in handling, 47-49
  checklist for handling the forgotten, 39, 41
  elderly people as, how to handle, 46
  handling, who do not have appointments, 43, 230
  hints for dealing with, 161
  keeping notes on, 28-29, 33, 35
  non-English speaking, how to handle, 46
  proper handling of, 230
  tips for screening, 44
  tips on greeting, 160-161
  tone of voice when dealing with, 29, 46-47
  see also Human Relations
Voice:
  improving diction and, 208
  tone of, and first impressions, 104, 106
  tone of, on the telephone, 50-51, 68-69

Voice *(cont'd)*
  tone of, when dealing with visitors, 104
  volume of, and first impressions, 104, 106

W

Webster's New World Dictionary of the American Language, 130
Women:
  checklist on common makeup don'ts, 212
  checklist on ways to enhance your appearance, 212-213
  clothing for, 210
  cosmetics and hairstyles for, 210-212
Women bosses, working with, 117, 119-120, 197-198
Women's Dress for Success Book, The, 213
Written communications:
  closings in, 75
  comma usage, 76-78
  examples of model letters, 81-91
  guidelines for composing letters, 72-73
  improving grammar skills, 75-81
  positive approach in, 74-75
  processing of incoming mail, 98-102
  quotation marks, use of, 80-81
  spelling and word division, 78-80
  tips for effective, 230-231
  type of stationery for, 92, 98